The Dead Cannot Reply

The Dead Cannot Reply

Suicide in Nineteenth- and Twentieth-Century English Literature

Aaron Botwick

BLOOMSBURY ACADEMIC
NEW YORK • LONDON • OXFORD • NEW DELHI • SYDNEY

BLOOMSBURY ACADEMIC
Bloomsbury Publishing Inc, 1359 Broadway, New York, NY 10018, USA
Bloomsbury Publishing Plc, 50 Bedford Square, London, WC1B 3DP, UK
Bloomsbury Publishing Ireland, 29 Earlsfort Terrace, Dublin 2, D02 AY28, Ireland

First published in the United States of America 2026

Cover design by Mary Kate Kelly | Typography by Fred Shallcrass
Cover image: Triptych, 1983, Francis Bacon © 2025 The Estate of Francis Bacon.
All rights reserved, DACS Images. Photographer: Prudence Cuming Associates Ltd

A catalog record for this book is available from the Library of Congress.

ISBN: HB: 979-8-7651-2881-7
ePDF: 979-8-7651-2883-1
eBook: 979-8-7651-2882-4

Typeset by Integra Software Services Pvt. Ltd.

For product safety-related questions, contact productsafety@bloomsbury.com.

For Bryn

Contents

Acknowledgments

First, I would like to thank everyone involved in the production of this book: my acquisitions editor at Bloomsbury Academic, Amy Martin; her assistant, Hali Han; Kumaraguru Elangovan, the project manager; Zeba Talkhani, the production manager; copyeditor Vidya Sundararajan; indexer Parthiban Dhinakaran; the typesetting team at Integra; the Bloomsbury Editorial Proofreading Team; Pete Woronkowicz, account manager at DACS, and Alan Baglia, account manager at Artists Rights Society, who helped me license Francis Bacon's *Triptych, 1983* for the cover image. The cover type was designed by my friend Fred Shallcrass, and the cover design is by my old friend Mary Kate Kelly, both done for free.

The Dead Cannot Reply began in graduate school, and I would like to thank Richard A. Kaye, who agreed to serve as my M.A. thesis supervisor, sight unseen, then later chaired both my orals and my dissertation committees. I started thinking about suicide as a research topic while taking Richard's course on Edwardian fiction. He suggested I take a look at *Women in Love*, and that began a long and fruitful relationship with Lawrence and the Lawrencians. The D.H. Lawrence Society of North America has been a source of continuous support—intellectual, professional, financial—since the 2018 D.H. Lawrence Virtual Conference for Graduate Students. I would like to thank, in particular, Holly A. Laird, who talked me through her research on modernism and suicide, and Nancy L. Paxton, who responded to the first paper on *Women in Love* with enthusiasm and encouragement (it was Nancy who suggested I take a look at Jung). Others who assisted me during the dissertation stage include Nico Israel, a reader on my dissertation committee, who did a line edit on the entire text, an act of grace I still cannot fathom; Tanya Agathocleous, also a reader on my dissertation committee, who told me I had not done enough to surprise her, a challenging but helpful criticism that I hope to have addressed in this book; and Dagmar Herzog, who gave me valuable leads on the subject of the death drive.

When I was an adjunct at City College, Elizabeth Mazzola offered me the chance to propose an English elective, and she remained supportive when I suggested one on literature and suicide. The students in that course, who read everything from the Vedas and the Hebrew Bible to Sylvia Plath and Sarah Kane, kept me intellectually honest. Katie Widdowson, Assistant Archives Officer at the U.K. Parliament, got me a facsimile of 4 George IV, c. 52, the Burial of Suicides Act of 1823. Chris Foster challenged my credulous reading of the final scene of *The Good Soldier*, a critique that unstuck my thinking on the matter.

A version of Chapter 4 appeared in *The D.H. Lawrence Review* 44, no. 2 (2019): 67–87. Thank you to the three anonymous readers from the *DHLR*—one did another line edit, a second act of grace—and the two from Bloomsbury Academic, who, in particular, helped me better frame the argument of the book. *The Dead Cannot Reply* was supported with funding from the PSC/CUNY Traditional A Research Award and the CUNY Book Completion Award. Moreover, my position as an assistant professor at Hostos Community College has provided me with the time and the resources, unavailable to many of my colleagues, to do this kind of work.

My parents are lifelong readers who have always encouraged their children to indulge in the pleasures of books. My father, Bill, began using the phrase "my son, the doctor" before I even began writing my dissertation, and my mother, Ruth, is probably at this very moment telling an exaggerated story about my professional triumphs. My older brother, Ben, gave me my first academic book—Thomas Allen Nelson's *Kubrick: Inside a Film Artist's Maze*—and my first glimpse into academic life. Brandishing his copy of *The Waste Land*, a Norton Critical Edition, he held the first twenty-odd pages between his fingers. "This is the poem," he said, then held the last two hundred fifty pages: "This is the commentary." I was enchanted.

Finally, I would like to thank Bryn Carter, my partner of thirteen years, to whom this book is dedicated. Your love, support, conversation, and criticism sustain me. I cannot imagine my life without you. You were there for graduate school, my first class, orals, the dissertation, the job market, the interview practice, the book proposal, and, of course, you were the first reader of this manuscript. I do all of this to show off for you.

Introduction

Suicide has long been explained through a combination of intellectual disciplines. The most prominent are three historical but porous categories: religious (it is the result of evil), sociological (it is the result of environment), and psychological (it is the result of personality). Martin Luther, for example, claimed that in all cases of voluntary death, "'tis the devil who has put the cord round their necks, or the knife to their throats."[1] The influence of religious explanations waned across the seventeenth and eighteenth centuries in favor of sociological and psychological ones. Sympathy for the victims and their survivors eclipsed condemnation for their actions, and the harshest punishments were abolished or underenforced. The professionalization of suicidology at the end of the nineteenth century formalized the distinction between sociology and psychology, and the work of Émile Durkheim and Sigmund Freud dominated interpretations of voluntary death throughout the twentieth century.

In *The Dead Cannot Reply*, I argue that this professionalization transformed the debate on suicide, shifting the emphasis from its effects to its causes. The main point of contention in the nineteenth century was the punishment, both human and divine, of the "self-murderer." Should suicides still be staked through the heart and buried at crossroads? Should the state continue to seize their assets? In the twentieth century, the question changed to motives. Why does someone choose death? Fiction, unbound by factual truth, offers the best forum to carry out these debates, to imagine not only the causes of suicide but also what it feels like to live in a suicidal mind. This book investigates how these questions were answered in the English imagination.

1 Martin Luther, "Table Talk," in *The Ethics of Suicide: Historical Sources*, ed. Margaret Pabst Battin (Oxford University Press, 2015), 244.

England had a reputation for high suicide rates. George Cheyne's *The English Malady* (1773) coined an enduring phrase, one that found a French counterpart in "la mort à l'anglaise."[2] The belief that the English were prone to suicide, later disproven, was repeated by figures as diverse as Voltaire,[3] Montesquieu,[4] John Wesley,[5] and Jack London.[6] Robert Blair called it "Our island's shame!" and Edward Young apostrophized, "O Britain, infamous for suicide!"[7] Thomas Jefferson explained that Americans were less vulnerable due to the weather: "It is our cloudless sky which has eradicated from our constitutions all disposition to hang ourselves, which we might otherwise have inherited from our English ancestors."[8] Boswell suggested as a method of prevention freezing the English in November.[9] In France, the government banned the gazettes from reporting on suicide, but in England, newspapers published the details of their deaths and sometimes the contents of their notes.[10] This no doubt influenced perceptions about national differences in suicide rates, but the belief in a national crisis, along with the English freedom of speech, enables us to better follow the trajectory of their ideas about what these deaths mean.

Suicide and Literature

While the subject has received increased attention over the last decade, fictional representations of suicide remain understudied, considering their ubiquity in the history of literature. The sheer volume of texts that depict suicides warrants, I believe, a brief sketch of its prevalence, though the following potted history should not be read as exhaustive and ends in the nineteenth century, where this book begins. The earliest known work of suicide literature is "Dispute between

2 Michael MacDonald and Terence R. Murphy, *Sleepless Souls: Suicide in Early Modern England* (Clarendon Press, 1990), 308.

3 Voltaire, "Philosophical Dictionary," in *The Ethics of Suicide*, 398–9.

4 Montesquieu, "The Spirit of the Laws," in *The Ethics of Suicide*, 395.

5 John Wesley, "Thoughts on Suicide," in *The Ethics of Suicide*, 404.

6 Barbara T. Gates, *Victorian Suicide: Mad Crimes and Sad Histories* (Princeton University Press, 1988), 156.

7 Quoted in Gates, *Victorian Suicide*, 23.

8 Thomas Jefferson, *The Writings of Thomas Jefferson Volume XI*, ed. Andrew A. Lipscomb (The Thomas Jefferson Memorial Association, 1904), 64.

9 MacDonald and Murphy, *Sleepless Souls*, 312.

10 Georges Minois, *History of Suicide: Voluntary Death in Western Culture*, trans. Lydia G. Cochrane (Johns Hopkins University Press, 1999), 287.

a man and his Ba" (*c*.1991–1802 BCE), a poetic fragment from the Egyptian Middle Kingdom. A man in despair longs for death, which prompts his *ba*, "the indwelling demonic power that controlled man's life," to threaten to leave.[11] This separation would mean annihilation for the man, as it would preclude the resurrection he desires. He begs his *ba* to remain with him, which it does: "I shall alight after you have become weary, and then we shall dwell together!"[12] The text is notable not only for its precedent but also for its psychological, rather than social, focus.

In the *Rāmāyana* (*c*.700 BCE–300 CE), Lakshmana drowns himself in the Sarayu River: "He stopped the activities of his senses and ceased to exhale."[13] Rāma announces that he wishes to join Lakshmana, and his silent, ritualized march into the Sarayu is accompanied by a crowd of chattering subjects who wish in turn "to follow Rāma to heaven."[14] There are five suicides in the Hebrew Bible, all military deaths. Samson destroys himself when he pulls down the Philistine temple (Judg. 16:30), and Ahitophel hangs himself after his plot against David fails (2 Sam. 17:23). A woman casts a millstone onto Abimelech's head, breaking his skull, and he orders his armor-bearer to kill him with his sword so others cannot say he was slain by a woman (Judg. 9:53). Saul loses a battle and orders the same, but his armor-bearer will not kill him, so he does it himself, and only then does the armor-bearer commit suicide (1 Sam. 31:4 and 1 Chron. 10:4). Finally, Zimri burns down his palace while he remains inside, ending a siege, his life, and his seven-day reign as king of Israel (1 Kgs 16:18). There are two suicides in the Apocrypha, both responses to antisemitism: Ptolemy takes poison when he is denounced as a traitor for showing justice to Jews (2 Macc. 14:41), and Razis falls on his sword rather than submit to Nicanor, who, "wishing to exhibit the enmity that he had for the Jews," sends five hundred soldiers to arrest him (2 Macc. 14:41).[15] Job, the most tested of the prophets, confides to a friend, "Oh that I might have my request; and that God would grant me the thing that I long for! Even that it would please God to destroy me; that he would let loose his hand, and cut me off!" (6:8-9). Job survives his test—there are no suicides of despair in the Hebrew Bible. There is one in the New Testament, Judas Iscariot, who betrays Christ, attempts to return his thirty pieces of silver, and then hangs himself. The

[11] Miriam Lichtheim, ed., *Ancient Egyptian Literature Volume I: The Old and Middle Kingdoms* (University of California Press, 1973), 135.

[12] Lichtheim, *Ancient Egyptian Literature Volume I*, 169.

[13] Vālmīki, *Rāmāyana*, trans. Arshia Sattar (Rowman & Littlefield, 2018), 525.

[14] Vālmīki, *Rāmāyana*, 527.

[15] *The Bible: Authorized King James Version with Apocrypha*, ed. Robert Carroll and Stephen Prickett (Oxford University Press, 2008).

suicide is only mentioned in one of the four canonical gospels, "The Gospel of Matthew" (*c.*75 CE). Still, by the Middle Ages, the suicide would become "Judas' trademark," and it is depicted in three of the four extant medieval mystery play cycles (the York, the Wakefield, and the N-Town).[16] In the *Qur'an* (*c.*644–56), Mohammad instructs his followers not to "kill (or destroy) yourselves," making it the only Abrahamic scripture to prohibit voluntary death (An-Nisā' 29).[17]

Suicide was central to the Attic tragedies of the fifth century BCE. Even excluding willing sacrifices, attempted suicides, and suicide ideation, Euripides wrote two: Phaedra and Evadne, Sophocles seven: Antigone, Eurydice, Haemon, Ajax, Jocasta, Heracles, and Deianeira. Elise P. Garrison characterizes these deaths as motivated by a desire "to avoid disgrace and preserve an honorable reputation; to avoid further suffering; to end grief; and to sacrifice oneself for a greater good."[18] Almost all occur off-stage, with a messenger reporting the details. Jocasta, for example, is found "hanging by the neck, cradled high in a woven noose, spinning, swinging back and forth"[19] The exceptions are Euripides's Evadne and Sophocles's Ajax: the audience watches Evadne leap into her husband's funeral pyre and Ajax fall on his sword—rare, direct depictions of violence on the Greek stage.

For centuries, these myths would populate the pool of sources from which authors drew their plots, ensuring that suicide remained a key theme of Roman and later European literature. Virgil has Queen Dido, separated from Aeneas, ascend a pyre and throw herself on her lover's sword in the *Aeneid* (25–19 BCE), and in the contemporaneous *Heroides* (25–16 BCE), Ovid writes her a suicide note: "[A] Trojan knife nestles in my lap; tears fall from my cheeks on its hammered steel blade / and soon it will be stained with my blood."[20] Ovid's *Metamorphoses* (8 CE) contains fifteen suicides, including those of Dido, Ajax, and Heracles.[21] Like Sophocles, Seneca the Younger leaves Deianeira to an offstage death, but in a departure from the Greek practice, his two other suicides, Phaedra and Jocasta, are enacted for the audience. His Jocasta, for example, cries, "Strike here, my hand, through this capacious womb, which bore my husband

16 Alexander Murray, *Suicide in the Middle Ages Volume II: The Curse on Self-Murder* (Oxford University Press, 2007), 328.
17 *The Holy Qur'an*, trans. Abdullah Yusuf Ali (Wordsworth, 2000).
18 Elise P. Garrison, *Groaning Tears: Ethical and Dramatic Aspects of Suicide in Greek Tragedy* (Brill, 1995), 2.
19 Sophocles, *The Three Theban Plays*, trans. Robert Fagles (Penguin, 1984), 237.
20 Ovid, *Heroides*, trans. Harold Isbell (Penguin, 1990), 64.
21 Saxby Pridmore and Zainab Abd Majeed, "The Suicides of *The Metamorphoses*," *Australasian Psychiatry* 19, no. 1 (February 2011), 24.

and my sons!" and then stabs herself.[22] Apuleius's *Metamorphoses* (*c*.200 CE), the only extant Roman novel, is in essence a series of suicides interrupted by a narrative: it chronicles seven completed suicides and seven attempts, in addition to the protagonist Lucius's three tries.[23]

Late in Murasaki Shikibu's *The Tale of Genji* (*c*.1021), considered the first modern novel, the princess Ukifune cannot choose between her two suitors and attempts to drown herself in the Uji River, leaving a note that reads, "With sighs of regret I cast away my life / Knowing that after my death my woeful name / Will flow onward, drifting in the shadows."[24] Petrarch considers the same dilemma as Hamlet in Sonnet 36 of *The Canzoniere* (1327–74): "If I thought that by death I would be lightened / of this amorous care that weighs me down, / by now, by my own hand I would have buried / these loathsome limbs of mine and that weight too."[25] Chaucer introduced iambic pentameter to English verse with *The Legend of Good Women* (*c*.1380–6), in which five of the ten good women (Cleopatra, Thisbe, Dido, Lucretia, and Phyllis) are classical suicides, all committed for love or honor. Dante sentenced self-murderers to the seventh circle of hell, entombed in gnarled thorn bushes and fed on by Harpies. "Like the rest, we shall return to claim our bodies," one tells the poet, "but never again to wear them—wrong it is / for a man to have again what he once cast off."[26] Dante makes an exception for Cato, who serves as the guardian to the gates of purgatory. Boccaccio's *The Decameron* (*c*.1348–53) contains five stories about suicide, all the result of thwarted love—in one, a woman "allow[s] herself to fall" out of an open window after being informed by her jealous husband that the "special dish" he has prepared for her is the heart of her lover.[27] *Le Morte d'Arthur* (1469–70) depicts a "damesel" in love with Lancelot who throws herself on his sword.[28] Notions of classical chivalry would continue to influence the meaning of self-murder into the sixteenth century.[29]

22 Seneca, *Tragedies*, trans. Frank Justus Miller (William Heinemann Ltd., 1938), 521.

23 See Andreas N. Michalopoulos, "Lucius' Suicide Attempts in Apuleius' 'Metamorphoses,'" *The Classical Quarterly* 52, no. 2 (2002), 538–48.

24 Murasaki Shikibu, *The Tale of Genji*, trans. Dennis Washburn (Norton, 2016), 1215. Emphasis in original.

25 Petrarch, *The Canzoniere or Rerum vulgarium framenta*, trans. Mark Musa (Indiana University Press, 1999), 1–4.

26 Dante, *The Divine Comedy Volume 1: Inferno*, trans. Mark Musa (Penguin, 1984), XIII, 103–5.

27 Giovanni Boccaccio, *The Decameron*, ed. and trans. G. H. McWilliam (Penguin, 1995), 351 and 352. This is 4–9. The other suicide stories are 4–1, 4–7, 4–8, and 5–8.

28 Sir Thomas Malory, "Le Morte Darthur," March 1469 to March 1470, MS 59678, The British Library, London, f.25v.

29 MacDonald and Murphy, *Sleepless Souls*, 95.

Edmund Spenser rehearses the arguments against suicide in *The Faerie Queene* (1590), and in both versions of Sir Philip Sidney's *Arcadia* (*c.*1580–90), most of the major characters attempt to kill themselves and quite a few succeed.[30] Shakespeare, of course, littered his stage with the bodies of suicides, and in this he only exaggerates the proclivities of his contemporaries: there were over two hundred on the English stage between 1580 and 1640, fifty-two written by Shakespeare.[31] These include Lady Macbeth, Cleopatra, Romeo and Juliet, Ophelia, Othello, and Brutus. Hamlet's question on the subject are the most famous words in the English language, a moment that Marjorie Garber argues "has come to define [...] the birth, in effect, of the modern subject, of modern subjectivity itself."[32] Christopher Marlowe (Dido, Bajazeth, Zabina, Agydas), Ben Jonson (Silius), John Webster (The Duchess), Thomas Kyd (Bel-imperia), Francis Beaumont and John Fletcher (Evadne, Amintor), and Thomas Middleton and William Rowley (De Flores) all wrote characters who kill themselves. Jean Racine's *Phèdre* (1677) concludes with Phèdre explaining her means of suicide: "The sword would have finished me already, / [... But] I wanted to tell you all my remorse / And go down to the dead a slower way. / I have taken, I have set in my burning veins / A poison which Medea brought to Athens."[33] In the religious allegory *Pilgrim's Progress* (1678), Hopeful talks Christian out of suicide; in *Paradise Lost* (1667; revised 1672), Adam Eve. Aphra Behn's royal slave, the eponymous *Oroonoko* (1688), makes a suicide pact with his lover, Imoinda.

Chikamatsu Monzaemon staged *The Love Suicides at Sonezaki* (1703) within three weeks of the events on which it is based.[34] Performed with puppets, *Sonezaki* "created a vogue for plays about lovers' suicides" as well as "a new genre of Japanese theater, the *sewamono*, or plays about contemporary life."[35] Donald Keane notes that the term *shinjū*, which he translates as *love suicide*, literally means *within the heart* and was associated with prostitutes who were forced to pledge their love for their customers, suicide being the ultimate evidence of that pledge.[36] In 1772,

30 Paul D. Green, "Doors to the House of Death: The Treatment of Suicide in Sidney's *Arcadia*," *The Sixteenth Century Journal* 10, no. 3 (Autumn 1979), 17–27.

31 Minois, *History of Suicide*, 149.

32 Marjorie Garber, *Shakespeare After All* (Anchor Books, 2004), 475.

33 Jean Racine, *Britannicus; Phaedra; Athaliah*, trans. C. H. Sisson (Oxford University Press, 2001), 1660–4.

34 Donald Keene, "The Love Suicides at Sonezaki," in *Masterworks of Asian Literature in Comparative Perspective*, ed. Barbara Stoler (Routledge, 1994), 521.

35 Keene, "Sonezaki," 521, 523–4.

36 Keene, "Sonezaki," 520–1.

the shogunate banned plays with *shinjū* in the title.[37] Alexander Pope elegized his "heap of dust" in "Elegy to the Memory of an Unfortunate Lady" (1717), as well as all who "act a lover's or a Roman's part."[38] *Roman* had long been synonym for honorable suicide—think of Horatio, who tells the dying Hamlet, "I am more an antique Roman than a Dane; / Here's yet some liquor left."[39] The final letter in Montesquieu's *Persian Letters* (1721) is a suicide note, and in Voltaire's *Candide* (1759), an old woman says, "A hundred times I wanted to kill myself, but still I loved life. This ridiculous weakness for living is perhaps one of our most fatal tendencies."[40] Jean-Jacques Rousseau stages a debate on the ethics of voluntary death in *Julie, or the New Heloise* (1761).

During the peak of the *Sturm und Drang* movement, Johann Wolfgang von Goethe made a secular religion out of suicide with *The Sorrows of Young Werther* (1774; revised 1787; translated into English 1779). The epistolary novella depicts the love of the title character for an unavailable woman, and when she marries, he shoots himself with his pistol. Readers were infatuated: seven different English translations were published between 1779 and 1809.[41] Werther inspired men to wear his signature buff-yellow waistcoat with knee-breeches and women to wear *Eau de Werther*.[42] A tableau, "Group of the Death of Werter [*sic*], attended by Charlotte and her family," was staged in a Fleet Street wax museum.[43] Byron called him "the first literary character in Europe,"[44] and Thackeray wrote a satire: "So he sighed and pined and ogled, / And his passion boiled and bubbled, / Till he blew his silly brains out, / And no more was by it troubled."[45] Madame de Staël claimed, "Werther has caused more suicides than the most beautiful woman in the world," and she was merely repeating the widely held belief that the character had inspired real suicides.[46] Goethe, troubled by this reaction,

[37] Margaret Pabst Battin, *The Ethics of Suicide: Historical Sources* (Oxford University Press, 2015), 380.

[38] Alexander Pope, *The Major Works*, ed. Pat Rogers (Oxford University Press, 2006), 147–8.

[39] William Shakespeare, *The Norton Shakespeare*, ed. Stephen Greenblatt, Walter Cohen, Suzanne Gossett, Jean E. Howard, Katharine Eisaman Maus, and Gordon McMullan (Norton, 2016), vii, 19–20.

[40] Voltaire, *Candide*, trans. Roger Pearson (Oxford University Press, 2006), 28.

[41] Orie W. Long, "English Translations of Goethe's *Werther*," *The Journal of English and Germanic Philology* 14, no. 2 (April 1915), 172.

[42] David Constantine, Introduction to *The Sorrows of Young Werther* (Oxford University Press, 2012), xxvii.

[43] Constantine, Introduction, 17.

[44] Quoted in Constantine, Introduction, 7.

[45] William Makepeace Thackeray, "Sorrows of Werther," in *The Humorous Poetry of the English Language, from Chaucer to Saxe*, ed. James Parton (Fields, Osgood & Company, 1870), 319.

[46] Quoted in Minois, *History of Suicide*, 268.

appended a poem to the 1775 second edition that read, "*Be a man, and do not follow me*."[47]

A. Alvarez writes that the Romantic poets "thought of suicide when they went to bed at night, and thought of it again in the morning when they shaved."[48] There is substantial evidence to support this claim. Keats begins "Ode to a Nightingale" (1819), "My heart aches [...] as though of hemlock I had drunk," and the speaker later recalls, "I have been half in love with easeful Death."[49] Byron's Manfred seeks "Oblivion, self-oblivion" in the Burmese Alps.[50] Frankenstein, perhaps the most enduring creation of English Romanticism, intends to commit suicide at the end of Mary Shelley's novel. When the death of a minor poet, Thomas Chatterton, was declared a suicide despite evidence to suggest otherwise, it became a *cause célèbre*. Wordsworth calls him "the marvellous Boy,"[51] Keats the "Dear Child of Sorrow! Son of Misery!"[52] In lines excised from later versions of "Monody on the Death of Chatterton" (1790), Coleridge writes, "But Chatterton! methinks I hear thy name [...] Athirst for Death I see thee drench the bowl!"[53] Deanna P. Koretsky has argued that this conventional Romantic suicide was reserved for white men: "to have the luxury of romanticizing suicide, the suicidal subject must first be legible as fully human."[54] Abolitionist literature that depicted the suicides of Black characters, such as John Bicknell and Thomas Day's poem "The Dying Negro" (1773), "fram[ed] the choice to die [...] as a sign of one's capacity to reason."[55] On Chatterton, Koretsky notes, "The reality of suicide is complicated; romantic suicide is decidedly less so."[56]

It seems fairly uncontroversial, then, to make the following two claims: first, suicide is one of the persistent tropes in the history of global literature, from early religious narratives to the modern novel. Second, there remains work to

[47] Stanley Corngold, Introduction to *The Sufferings of Young Werther* (Norton, 2012), 7. Emphasis in original.

[48] A. Alvarez, *The Savage God: A Study of Suicide* (Penguin, 1974), 231.

[49] John Keats, "Ode to a Nightingale," in *The Major Works*, ed. Elizabeth Cook (Oxford University Press, 2008), 1, 3, and 52.

[50] Lord Byron, "Manfred," in *The Major Works*, ed. Jerome J. McGann (Oxford University Press, 2008), 144.

[51] William Wordsworth, "Resolution and Independence," in *The Major Works*, ed. Stephen Gill (Oxford University Press, 2008), 44.

[52] Keats, "Oh Chatterton! How Very Sad Thy Fate!" in *The Major Works*, 2.

[53] Samuel Taylor Coleridge, *The Complete Poems of Samuel Taylor Coleridge*, ed. William Keach (Penguin, 1997), 3, 6.

[54] Deanna P. Koretsky, *Death Rights: Romantic Suicide, Race, and the Bounds of Liberalism* (State University of New York Press, 2021), 96.

[55] Koretsky, *Death Rights*, 5.

[56] Koretsky, *Death Rights*, 125.

be done. This book is an attempt to answer in part Andrew Bennett's call for a project of "literary suicidology."[57]

Vocabulary and Definition

Suicide is the most prevalent term used for the action in modern English. Sir Thomas Browne, inspired by the same neoclassicism as Montesquieu and Voltaire, coined it in his revision of *Religio Medici* (1643). The unauthorized edition of 1642 condemns those "that can allow a man to be his own *Assaßine*, and so highly extoll the end of Cato," while the 1643 first edition reads "[...] the end and suicide of *Cato*."[58] The word soon spread to French, Spanish, Italian, and Portuguese.[59] It was popular enough to be included in Edward Phillips's *The New World of English Words* (1658), though Phillips advocates for a false etymology: "I had rather [the word] should be derived from *sus*, a Sow, then from the Pronown *sui* [...] as if it were a Swinish part for a man to kill himself."[60] In fact, it is derived from the Latin *sui*, or self, and *cædo*, to kill. Kelly McGuire points out that this "constitutes 'bad Latin' in its unorthodox use of a pronoun as a prefix,"[61] and Romans instead used the phrases *sibi mortem consciscere* (to procure one's own death), *veneno mortem sibi consciscere* (to poison oneself), *vim sibi inferre* (to cause violence to oneself), *sua manu cadere* (to fall by one's own hand), and *mors voluntaria* (voluntary death).[62] Johnson's 1755 dictionary defines suicide as "Self-murder; the horrid crime of destroying one's self."[63] Despite the ungenerous lexicographers, *suicide* is a more neutral term than some of its predecessors, including *self-murder*, as it removes most of its criminal connotations. Moreover, it distances speakers from the immediacy of their native languages—"Remarkable how the [L]atinized forms always suck the

57 Andrew Bennett, *Suicide Century: Literature and Suicide from James Joyce to David Foster Wallace* (Cambridge University Press, 2017), 21.

58 Sir Thomas Browne, *Religio Medici* (Andrew Crooke, 1642), 81; Sir Thomas Browne, *Religio Medici* (Andrew Crooke, 1643), 98. Emphases in original.

59 MacDonald and Murphy, *Sleepless Souls*, 146.

60 Edward Phillips, ed., *The New World of English Words* (E. Tyler, 1658), c2.

61 Kelly McGuire, *Dying to Be English: Suicide Narratives and National Identity, 1721–1814* (Pickering & Chatto, 2012), 2.

62 William Wynn Westcott, *Suicide: Its History, Literature, Jurisprudence, Causation, and Prevention* (H. K. Lewis, 1885), 31–2.

63 Samuel Johnson, *A Dictionary of the English Language Volume II* (W. Strahan, 1855), SUG-SUI.

reality out of something," writes Jean Améry.[64] Like Améry, I prefer *voluntary death*, which further removes judgmental connotations ("to commit suicide" paralleling "to commit murder" or "to commit sin") but will use both for the sake of simplicity, along with contemporaneous terms when appropriate.

Here is my definition of *suicide*: any action or inaction that is taken in order to die within a short period of time. Refusing to eat food or drink water would, so long as it is done with the intention of dying, fall under this definition. What Karl Menninger calls "suicide by inches," or reckless behavior such as drinking and driving or excessive drug use, would not, since these deaths do not necessarily occur within a short period of time.[65] It also excludes the soldier who jumps on the grenade to save his comrades, since dying in this case is not an intention but a consequence. The same logic applies to kamikaze pilots and so-called suicide bombers.

Chapters

What did Victorians think about suicide? Religious tracts, legal commentaries, newspaper articles, poems, and three-decker novels all shaped the discourse. In Chapter 1, "Common Graves," I argue that these texts facilitated an understanding of suicide as a public event, one whose meaning is located in its meaning for others. The religious argument claims that the body belongs not to the individual but to God; the legal that it belongs to the crown; and the literary that it belongs to the readers. The causes are understood. It is the consequences of suicide, the effects, that are contested: the degree of divine, legal, or narrative punishment. In this context, fictional suicides are often peripheral, the means of resolving a narrative problem. Bertha Mason, for example, leaps from Thornfield Hall and liberates Edward Rochester to marry Jane Eyre. Because the emphasis is on the ends these deaths achieve, and because their means are clear and uncomplicated, I call this the *teleology of suicide*.

Consequently, Victorian fiction was largely unconcerned with what Bennett calls "the phenomenology, the lived experience [...] of suicide."[66] The subject is

[64] Jean Améry, *On Suicide: A Discourse on Voluntary Death*, trans. John D. Barlow (Indiana University Press, 1999), 2.

[65] Quoted in Frank Giordano Jr., *"I'd Have My Life Unbe": Thomas Hardy's Self-destructive Characters* (University of Alabama Press, 1984), 36.

[66] Bennett, *Suicide Century*, 4.

the witness, not the victim, and therefore the thoughts of the suicidal character are not especially relevant to these narratives. One exception is the villain. At the end of the century, Marie Corelli and Robert Louis Stevenson attempted a full account of the experience of suicide, abstaining from off-stage deaths or free indirect discourse and instead writing direct testimony. Both the title character in *The Sorrows of Satan* (1895) and one of the title characters in *Strange Case of Dr. Jekyll and Mr. Hyde* (1886) compose extended suicide notes that precede their deaths by only moments. In Chapter 2, "The Last Word," I argue that Corelli and Stevenson create a window of permissiveness for readers to imagine the experience of suicide in a historical context where voluntary death was not condemned but not condoned. Only a border character like a villain can provide such a direct view, free of guilt over immorality and fear of contamination.

By the end of the nineteenth century, the teleological explanations of suicide that characterized Victorian fiction became untenable. The alleviation of punishments, the professionalization of coroners, the decreased influence of juries, and reduced coverage in the press all decreased public exposure to the debates on suicide. Fear and an "abdication of the community" made modern death "invisible."[67] In Chapter 3, "Make It Vague," I argue that one major modernist response to these changes was to view suicide as a problem of epistemology, as a failure of knowing. Did the subject choose death? If so, why? Once causes, rather than effects, are contested, they become fertile narrative ground. I read John Galsworthy's *The Man of Property* (1906) as a hinge moment, since the author revised an explicit suicide to an "accident," and follow with a reading of Ford Madox Ford's *The Good Soldier* (1915), a novel that takes as its subject the multiple, contradictory, and unresolved causes of suicide.

In Chapter 4, "Entering Other Lives," I consider an alternative to the epistemological failure in Galsworthy and Ford: Septimus Warren-Smith in Virginia Woolf's *Mrs. Dalloway* (1925). The causes of his death are clear. The problem is what follows: in the novel's penultimate scene, Clarissa envisions Septimus's suicide and experiences an epiphany. As a result, she feels "somehow very like him."[68] Should we consider this epiphany, this moment of communion, genuine? The answer has great bearing on whether Woolf's choice to experiment with stream-of-consciousness meets the demands of her subject matter. As a

[67] Philippe Ariès, *The Hour of Our Death*, trans. Helen Weaver (Barnes & Noble Books, 2000), 612 and 559.

[68] Virginia Woolf, *Mrs. Dalloway*, ed. Anne E. Fernald (Cambridge University Press, 2014), 166.

pseudo-witness to his suicide, Clarissa stands in for the reader. Her vicarious experience of his death is not unlike our own. If her epiphany is genuine, then fiction can offer the illusion of unmediated intimacy that real life denies us.

Throughout the twentieth century, suicide discourse was dominated by two disciplines: sociology and psychology. Margaret Pabst Battin calls it "the time of [Sigmund] Freud and [Émile] Durkheim."[69] Chapter 5, "The Suicidal Type," is about sociology. Early practitioners such as Durkheim and Enrico Morselli are concerned with correlation and tend to dismiss questions of causality and, in consequence, questions of agency. I argue that detective fiction more readily adopted the sociological model of the "suicidal type" than its progenitors. When used as a plot device, the body of a suicide, either authentic or staged, is one of the few undisputed truths of Golden Age detective fiction, and a sociologist's observation (the old commit suicide more than the young) becomes a detective's rule (she didn't kill herself; she was young). Where Durkheim and his contemporaries demonstrate shared characteristics among suicidal people, Hercule Poirot and Lord Peter Wimsey transform them into universal laws of human nature.

The main contribution of psychoanalysis to suicide discourse is the concept of the *death drive*, which Freud defines as a conservative impulse to return to an earlier state of things, the earliest of which is nonexistence. D. H. Lawrence never read Freud, but he was close with several psychoanalysts, and the subject permeated the culture. In Chapter 6, "The Gospel of the Death Drive," I argue that Lawrence's concept of *blood knowledge* is a variation on Freud's death drive. With blood knowledge, which he opposes to *mental knowledge*, Lawrence advocates for the use of instinct over intellect. He argues that destruction, conflict, and rupture are necessary for both personal and cultural rebirth. But where Freud sees the death drive as a neurotic symptom produced by the disease of civilization, Lawrence sees blood knowledge as the cure. Through a reading of his poem "Eloi, Eloi, Lama Sabachthani?" (1915) and his novel *Women in Love* (1920), I argue that Lawrence viewed suicide as part of this cure, as a component of an ancient, primitivist, and cyclical rite of history that offered humanity salvation through destruction. Lawrence revives the teleological explanations of the Victorians with a crucial difference: its purpose is now inscrutable to the witness and the reader, who are both limited by the boundaries of mental knowledge.

[69] Margaret Pabst Battin, ed., *The Ethics of Suicide: Historical Sources* (Oxford University Press, 2015), 476.

1

Common Graves: Victorian Fiction and the Teleology of Suicide

In his popular and much-illustrated poem "The Bridge of Sighs" (1844), Thomas Hood instructs his reader to treat the body of a drowned woman, "One more Unfortunate" (1), with "Loving, not loathing" (14).[1] He acknowledges that hers was "evil behaviour" (104), but we are to make "no deep scrutiny / Into her mutiny" (21–2) and instead leave "Her sins to her savior" (106). The reader is asked to pick up her body, close her eyelids, and fix her hair. We are told to wipe her "oozing" lips (30), "smooth" her limbs (87), and "cross" her arms over her breast to simulate prayer (100). The speaker does not reveal any direct knowledge of the victim, but he imagines her standing on Waterloo Bridge, shivering and illuminated by the lights of the city, and he demands we do the same: "Picture it—think of it, / Dissolute Man! / Lave in it, drink of it, / Then, if you can!" (76–9). The image of the drowned woman was a common artistic conceit in the Victorian era—there was even an idiom, "making a hole in the water"—and the assumption at inquests would be that an unmarried woman who killed herself had been seduced and abandoned.[2]

Hood's portrait of voluntary death draws on a range of disciplines that shaped suicide discourse in the nineteenth century. *Evil*, *sins*, and *savior* are all religious, as is the command to cross the Unfortunate's arms. Christian theologians have long argued that the body is a vessel, the property of God, and therefore, suicide is its theft. Nevertheless, the speaker does not conceive of suicide as sinful, and his direction to place her in a position of devotion implies redemption, as do

[1] Thomas Hood, *Poems* (Henry Frowde, 1907), 167–70. All subsequent references are to line numbers and noted parenthetically in the text.

[2] Olive Anderson, *Suicide in Victorian and Edwardian England* (Oxford University Press, 1987), 210 and 57.

the baptismal associations of her plunge into and emergence from the Thames. The Unfortunate achieves what L. J. Nicoletti calls a "peaceful martyrdom," but she is a martyr to a social rather than a religious cause.[3] The tone is polemical, written in the second person, and comprised short, hectoring lines that demand the reader treat the woman with tenderness rather than scorn. Her death is not her failure but ours. The reader is identified as a "Dissolute Man," the implication that our behavior, our debauchery, is responsible for these tragedies. Thus, "The Bridge of Sighs" is consistent with Barbara Gates's argument that from 1822 to 1898, "stands against self-destruction would weaken" and "existential and social interpretations of suicide would increase."[4]

Still, despite the gesture of sympathy, the Unfortunate is not the real subject of the poem. "The Bridge of Sighs" is less concerned with the woman who leaped into the Thames than with the body that was recovered from the river. The title refers not to the Unfortunate, but to her means of suicide, the implied means of many. Her name is a capitalized adjective, an adjective that denotes fate rather than choice. The kind of character arc that we might expect from a narrative poem is reserved for the reader: the speaker demands we drink of her misery and then transform our moral outrage into self-examination. The Unfortunate's story is over before the poem begins. We are the ones who need to *lave* (or wash); we are the ones awaiting baptism. Our name, Dissolute Man, denotes both agency and personhood. The Waterloo Bridge is a site for our edification. When John Cobley wrote, "The life of Chatterton is [...] public property," he could have added that his death is, too.[5]

In the following chapter, I will argue that "The Bridge of Sighs" is representative of nineteenth-century English literature and its depiction of voluntary death. Religious tracts, legal commentaries, broadsheets, and three-decker novels all facilitated an understanding of suicide as a public event, one whose meaning is located in its meaning for others. The religious argument claims that the body belongs not to the individual but to God; the legal that it belongs to the crown; and the literary that it belongs to readers. The causes are understood. It is the effects that are contested: the degree of divine, legal, or social punishment. In

[3] L. J. Nicoletti, "Downward Mobility: Victorian Women, Suicide, and London's 'Bridge of Sighs,'" *Literary London: Interdisciplinary Studies in the Representation of London* 2, no. 1 (March 2004).

[4] See Barbara T. Gates, *Victorian Suicide: Mad Crimes and Sad Histories* (Princeton University Press, 1988), 15.

[5] Quoted in L. J. Nicoletti, "Morbid Topographies: Placing Suicide in Victorian London," in *A Mighty Mass of Brick and Smoke: Victorian and Edwardian Representations of London*, ed. Lawrence Phillips (Rodopi, 2007), 26.

fiction, suicide is often peripheral, a component that helps move the gears of the plot, significant for its consequences. When Mirah Lapidoth attempts to drown herself, she convinces Daniel Deronda to "take part in the battle of the world";[6] when Bertha Mason leaps from the roof of Thornfield Hall, she liberates Edward Rochester and enables him to marry Jane Eyre; and when a parade of villains hang, shoot, and poison themselves, their deaths serve as punctuation marks on their turpitude, reinforcing the moral order of the universe in which their stories are set. For the most part, Victorian novelists ignore the thoughts and the behavior that precipitate a suicide, the free indirect discourse of these characters, what Andrew Bennett calls "the phenomenology, the lived experience [...] of suicide."[7] Because the emphasis is on their effects, and because their causes are straightforward and uncomplicated—a rhetorical form of entombment, which resolves and silences doubt—I call this phenomenon the *teleology of suicide*. "The Bridge of Sighs" does not debate why the Unfortunate chose death. That matter is settled. It debates the reaction her suicide should provoke in us.

Suicides as Public Property

In England, much of the culture coalesced to facilitate a public understanding of suicide. After the so-called Age of Martyrs, the Church established a consistent position against voluntary death. The Council of Gaudix (305) removed the names of suicides from the list of martyrs, and the Council of Carthage (348) condemned these deaths as evil. The Council of Arles (452) determined that suicide is the result of diabolical possession, but it also promulgated the first canon law on the subject, which concerns social rather than divine relationships: masters should not be reproached for the suicides of their slaves. As for the suicides themselves, many of the early ecclesiastical laws punished them with silence. The Council of Orleans (533) denied offerings on behalf of suicides and funerals for criminal suicides. The Council of Braga (561) extended the prohibition on funerals to all suicides. Hence Ophelia is buried without a requiem—"We should profane the service of the dead," says the priest, who is already uncomfortable leaving "her virgin crants" in a churchyard rather than

6 George Eliot, *Daniel Deronda*, ed. Graham Handley (Oxford University Press, 2014), 155. All subsequent references are noted parenthetically in the text.

7 Andrew Bennett, *Suicide Century: Literature and Suicide from James Joyce to David Foster Wallace* (Cambridge University Press, 2017), 4.

"ground unsanctified."[8] The Council of Toledo (693) went further and decreed that both suicides and attempted suicides should be excommunicated. The punishment for suicide was more severe than the punishment for murder, which constituted a fine.[9]

Christian writers have long emphasized a communal stake in the body of the subject. In the Epistle to the Philippians, Paul confesses that he has "a desire to depart, and to be with Christ; which is far better," but he recognizes that he is more valuable alive, the better to "continue with you all for your furtherance and joy of faith" (1:25).[10] The need to proselytize necessitates a proscription of suicide; the Macedonians have a claim on Paul that forces him to abandon thoughts of self-destruction. Justin Martyr elaborates on the Pauline argument, writing that suicide opposes the will of God because "no one would be born and be instructed in the divine doctrines."[11] In other words, a suicide has abandoned their religious obligation to procreate. Augustine, who wanted to dissuade would-be martyrs, establishes the basis for much subsequent Christian thought on the subject when he argues for a reading of Mosaic Law that implies prohibition: "Thou shalt not kill," because it excludes the conditional "thy neighbor," includes thyself.[12] Note that Augustine grounds his reasoning in a commandment that regulates man's relationship to man, in contrast to the Jewish tradition, which finds a prohibition of suicide in man's relationship to the divine: "God blessed Noah and his sons, and said to them [...] 'But for your own life-blood I will require a reckoning'" (Gen. 9:1, 5).[13] In *Summa Theologica* (1265–74), Thomas Aquinas lists three reasons suicide is unlawful. The second is that "every thing that is a part belongs to the whole [...] every man is part of a community [...] he who kills himself injures the community." For Aquinas, suicide is a theft from the group—the word *community* echoes like a refrain throughout this passage—and the group is its victim. In eschewing Paul's proselytization argument, he

[8] William Shakespeare, *The Norton Shakespeare*, ed. Stephen Greenblatt, Walter Cohen, Suzanne Gossett, Jean E. Howard, Katharine Eisaman Maus, and Gordon McMullan (Norton, 2016), vi, 215, 211, and 208.

[9] Georges Minois, *History of Suicide: Voluntary Death in Western Culture*, trans. Lydia G. Cochrane (Johns Hopkins University Press, 1999), 30.

[10] *The Bible: Authorized King James Version with Apocrypha*, ed. Robert Carroll and Stephen Prickett (Oxford University Press, 2008).

[11] Justin Martyr, "The Second Apology," in *The Ethics of Suicide: Historical Sources*, ed. Margaret Pabst Battin (Oxford University Press, 2015), 151.

[12] Augustine, *City of God*, trans. Henry Bettenson (Penguin, 2004), 31.

[13] Margaret Pabst Battin, ed., *The Ethics of Suicide: Historical Sources* (Oxford University Press, 2015), 27. Translation from *Tanakh: The Holy Scriptures: New Translation According to the Traditional Hebrew Text* (The Jewish Publication Society, 1988).

secularizes this collective claim on the suicide, even citing "the Philosopher," the pagan Aristotle, for confirmation of his position.[14]

Many influential post-Reformation theologians would adopt the same arguments. The Stuart preacher John Adams writes that "self-Murther [...] may prove destructive to the very Being of Society." Since it deprives punishments of their threats, it "void[s] all Obligation to Humane Laws" and "no Law would signify any thing."[15] For Adams, the prohibition of suicide is the foundation of all social regulations. *Self-murder*, by this point a legal term, dates to at least 1570 in English (*OED*). The word denotes an interpersonal rather than a private act; it implies a public cost. The dissenter Caleb Fleming argues that suicide rejects "the very foundation of social virtue," Christ's commandment to "love thy neighbor as thyself." To "capitally abuse ourselves" is "high-treason, not only against the sovereignty of the universal Lord, but against the laws of human society."[16] Fleming is notable in his use of Christian rather than Mosaic text and for reversing the traditional direction in which we read this commandment: suicide is prohibited because one must *love thyself as [one loves] thy neighbor*. It is a social commandment, and his euphemism for suicide, "capitally abuse ourselves," employs the language of the crown, not the language of the Lord.

English law followed the Aquinian argument, and suicide is handled exhaustively in *On the Laws and Customs of England* (*c*.1210–68). Attributed to Henry de Bracton, the authors of this legal commentary argue that suicide is comparable to murder, even if victim and assailant are the same: "Just as man may commit felony by slaying another so may he do so by slaying himself, the felony is said to be done to himself."[17] In the next comprehensive account of English law, William Blackstone's *Commentaries on the Laws of England* (1765–9), Blackstone praises the wisdom of the English legal system for prohibiting suicide as the perpetrator is guilty not only of spiritual but also "temporal" offense "against the king, who hath an interest in the preservation of all his subjects."[18] For Blackstone, like Aquinas, suicide is not only murder but also theft, albeit from the monarchy rather than the community. The argument spread to other disciplines. The political philosopher William Godwin wrote that "we are but

[14] Thomas Aquinas, "Summa Theologica," in *The Ethics of Suicide*, 229.

[15] John Adams, "An Essay Concerning Self-Murther," in *The Ethics of Suicide*, 385. See also Minois, *History of Suicide*, 189.

[16] Caleb Fleming, "A Dissertation upon the Unnatural Crime of Self-Murder," in *The Ethics of Suicide*, 402.

[17] Henry de Bracton, "On the Laws and Customs of England," in *The Ethics of Suicide*, 221 and 220.

[18] William Blackstone, "Commentaries on the Laws of England," in *The Ethics of Suicide*, 419.

one, and the persons nearly or remotely interested in our possible usefulness innumerable." The suicide has no right to his life, which is "so much wealth to be put to the account of the general stock."[19] The mathematician Richard Hey went so far as to ventriloquize the voice of the suicide, whom he imagined to be contemptuous of social obligations: "I consign to oblivion those dull maxims; which, under the title of Virtue, would teach me to distract myself by an assiduous attention to the rights and interests of others, instead of giving myself freely to my own gratification."[20]

From 1194, English coroners investigated accidental deaths, homicides, suicides and, after the mid-nineteenth century, all deaths in asylums, prisons, and on railways.[21] The investigation of suicides was not professionalized until the twentieth century, and the inquiry was "a peculiarly open one," even "a public drama."[22] Coroners worked part-time and required no professional qualifications.[23] Most were solicitors, some the children of "local dynasties."[24] Until 1888, they were elected rather than appointed, and by 1893, fewer than half were members of the Coroners' Society founded almost fifty years earlier in 1846.[25] In *Bleak House* (1852–3), Charles Dickens writes, "The coroner frequents more public-houses than any man alive. The smell of sawdust, beer, tobacco-smoke, and spirits, is inseparate in his vocation from death in its most awful shapes."[26] Coroners had "considerable latitude" in their management of the inquest rooms, which needed to hold as many as twenty-five people. Those present included the twelve members of the jury, the witnesses, and sometimes representatives for the relatives, insurance companies, and the police.[27] Coroner's juries were male, land-owning, middle-class, and, unlike other juries, needed no professional qualifications.[28] The body of the victim would be on view in a separate room.[29] Olive Anderson describes the trials as "irretrievably associated with undignified proceedings which went on in hired rooms in public houses, before very humble

19 William Godwin, "Enquiry Concerning Political Justice," in *The Ethics of Suicide*, 455.
20 Richard Hey, "Dissertation on Suicide," in *The Ethics of Suicide*, 442.
21 Victor Bailey, *"This Rash Act": Suicide Across the Life Cycle in the Victorian City* (Stanford University Press, 1998), 6, 38.
22 Anderson, *Suicide in Victorian and Edwardian England*, 223, 255.
23 Anderson, *Suicide in Victorian and Edwardian England*, 24, 28.
24 Bailey, *This Rash Act*, 38.
25 Anderson, *Suicide in Victorian and Edwardian England*, 39 and 17.
26 Charles Dickens, *Bleak House*, ed. Stephen Gill (Oxford University Press, 1998), 159–60.
27 Bailey, *This Rash Act*, 38 and 45.
28 Anderson, *Suicide in Victorian and Edwardian England*, 28.
29 Bailey, *This Rash Act*, 45.

jurors (who might sometimes be allowed to solace themselves with beer and tobacco), amidst the coming and going of stray cats, dogs, infants, and members of the public."[30] The scene resembles a circus as much as it does the investigation of a crime. The public had access to the levers of power, and it was the public that decided what was to be done with the body and the property of a suicide. Victor Bailey writes that "the essence of inquest practice was public participation and assent."[31]

English juries returned three verdicts on suicide. *Felo de se* ("felon of himself") was the harshest. Offenders were ruled *compos mentis*, able to distinguish good from evil, and therefore to have willed their own deaths. Until 1882, these were buried in unconsecrated ground, and until 1870, they were penalized, like all felons, with the seizure of their property, often leaving their dependents ruined. In his diary, Samuel Pepys records an attempt to protect the estate of his cousin's husband after he attempted to drown himself: "my cozen did endeavour to remove what she could of plate out of the house, and desired me to take my flagons; which I was glad of."[32] A second verdict, *non compos mentis* (or "temporary insanity"), relieved suicides of both punishments. Their bodies were interred on the north side of the churchyard with executed felons, excommunicates, and unbaptized infants.[33] This is where Heathcliff and Catherine are interred, after refusing food, in *Wuthering Heights* (1847).[34] When juries did not have enough information to make either determination, for example when the victim was a stranger, a third verdict was returned: "state of mind unknown." Coroners and juries become more lenient after the Restoration: in the 1660s, fewer than 7 percent of suicides were ruled *non compos mentis*; from 1770 to 1800, 97 percent were.[35] *Felo de se* was thereafter reserved for criminals, foreigners, and other social outcasts.[36] The English had long been divided on forfeiture, especially as property ownership became central to their national identity, and many were willing to manipulate the system to assist families of the deceased. Bailey documents a case where the coroner wrote that the victim attempted "to hang himself & died from fright," another where the jury returned the verdict "died by visitation of God after

[30] Anderson, *Suicide in Victorian and Edwardian England*, 33.
[31] Bailey, *This Rash Act*, 47.
[32] Samuel Pepys, "Diary," in *The Ethics of Suicide*, 313.
[33] Michael MacDonald and Terence R. Murphy, *Sleepless Souls: Suicide in Early Modern England* (Clarendon Press, 1990), 213.
[34] See Gates, *Victorian Suicide*, 10–11.
[35] MacDonald and Murphy, *Sleepless Souls*, 121, 133.
[36] Minois, *History of Suicide*, 284–5.

cutting his throat," and a third where a woman, Mary Wiles, drowned herself and her six-month-old daughter, Eliza. Wiles was found *non compos mentis* for the suicide but guilty of the felonious, "willful murder" of Eliza.[37] The high frequency of *non compos mentis* verdicts was a point of contention for some critics, who believed its overuse had eliminated the force of punishment. John Wesley, for example, complained, "If he is brought in insane, he is excused, and the law does not affect him. By this means it is totally eluded; for the juries constantly bring him in insane. So the law is not of the least effect, though the farce of a trial still continues."[38] Nevertheless, suicide remained a crime until 1961, and verdicts of *felo de se* were returned as late as the First World War.[39]

Ritual punishments were severe and executed in front of an audience. For centuries, the bodies of suicides were dragged to the gallows and hung face down before being thrown into ditches and highways for animals to eat, a practice that survived as late as 1598 in Edinburgh and 1749 in Paris.[40] Suicides were also staked through the heart, pinioned to their graves, and buried by torchlight between nine and midnight at crossroads.[41] Thomas Hardy records this death practice in "The Grave by the Handpost" (1897), and Bram Stoker immortalized it in *Dracula* (1897), which would incorporate the stake-through-the-heart into another living dead tradition. These customs were appropriated from pre-Christian societies and were meant to prevent revenants from returning home, as the crossroads would scramble their orientation.[42] Like those of all violent deaths, the soul of a suicide was "apt to wander."[43] The canons and liturgy did not mandate the desecration of bodies, but ministers in the Church of England "regarded them as essential aspects of the punishment of the sin of self-murder" and ignored their pagan origins.[44] Since there was no ecclesiastical legislation on the burial of self-murders, these were "genuine popular customs."[45] The ritual asks the public to serve as witnesses to a kind of postmortem execution, as juries at their burials, and audiences were participants in the drama of a suicide.

[37] Bailey, *This Rash Act*, 61, 72.
[38] John Wesley, "*Thoughts on Suicide*," in *The Ethics of Suicide*, 404.
[39] Minois, *History of Suicide*, 297.
[40] Wynn Westcott, *Suicide: Its History, Literature, Jurisprudence, Causation, and Prevention* (H. K. Lewis, 1885), 198–9.
[41] Michael MacDonald, "The Medicalization of Suicide in England: Laymen, Physicians, and Cultural Change, 1500–1870," *The Milbank Quarterly* 67 (1989), 69.
[42] MacDonald and Murphy, *Sleepless Souls*, 6.
[43] Anderson, *Suicide in Victorian and Edwardian England*, 233.
[44] MacDonald, "The Medicalization of Suicide in England," 71.
[45] MacDonald and Murphy, *Sleepless Souls*, 19–20.

Bailey records two cases where women required police protection from crowds enraged by their responsibility for a suicide,[46] and the funeral of Mary Wiles was "disturbed" by a number of women who found her husband responsible for her death, despite a coroner's exoneration.[47] The passage of 4 George IV, *c.* 52 in 1823 required that coroners "shall give Directions for the private Interment of the Remains of such Person [...] without any Stake being driven through the Body of such Person."[48]

Suicide narratives thrived in the press, even after the relaxation of laws and moral attitudes, and suicides were reported alongside divorces, bankruptcies, and other local indignities. Contributors included newspaper reporters, newspaper readers, judges and juries, coroners, physicians, religious leaders, poets, novelists, and, in some instances, the suicides themselves. "A good suicide was almost as gripping as a good murder," writes Anderson, "and far more interesting than most fatal accidents."[49] Here, for example, is a complete article from the February 14, 1891, edition of the *Jersey Weekly Press and Independent*:

> An inquest was held at Hampstead to-day, on the body of Kate Carter, aged 15, domestic servant of Netherwood-street, West Hampstead. The girl's mutilated body was found on the Midland Railway, near Cricklewood Station last Thursday night. Evidence showed that the girl's late master and mistress had spoken to her about gossiping, and this appears to have upset her, as she feared they would write to her stepfather. The jury found she committed suicide while of unsound mind.[50]

The address of the deceased, her professional circumstances, and the personal details that precipitated her death are all available for perusal. With an especial touch of cruelty, the author even reveals information that the suicide may have been meant to protect: Kate Carter's stepfather is likely to hear about her gossiping now, along with much of the newspaper's readership. She was not alone. In 1893, when a Nottingham laborer named Chambers hanged himself, *The Morning Post* noted that he was "completely dressed in his wife's garments, and even [had] her earrings in his ears."[51] In 1897, when the eleven-year-old

[46] Bailey, *This Rash Act*, 3, 202.
[47] Bailey, *This Rash Act*, 72, 78.
[48] "An Act to Alter and Amend the Law Relating to the Interment of the Remains of Any Person Found *Felo de se*," July 8, 1823.
[49] Anderson, *Suicide in Victorian and Edwardian England*, 195.
[50] "SUICIDE," *The Jersey Weekly Press and Independent*, February 14, 1891.
[51] "EXTRAORDINARY SUICIDE," *The Morning Post*, August 11, 1893.

Mary Paine drank two mouthfuls of morphine, *The Evening Telegraph and Star* reported, following a section titled "CHIT-CHAT," that Mary was "of weak intellect, and was in the habit of telling falsehoods and stealing." The author adds without further comment that her mother "died in a lunatic asylum."[52] In each case, there is no compunction about pilfering the intimate details of the dead. An article in *The Falkirk Herald and Midland Counties Journal* goes so far as the view suicide as a public nuisance, reporting on an alleged response to the Italian "fad" of using express trains as an instrument of death: the "suicide catcher [...] is placed in front of the locomotive like the American cowcatcher, and it scoops up the person who tries to use the engine for his own unpleasant purposes." A solution for "vexed" commuters.[53]

Victorian suicide discourse was both multivocal and absorbent. Ideas about voluntary death formed something of a harmonious collage, in which amateur and professional beliefs derived from (among others) religion, the law, and literature supplemented rather than invalidated one another. Furthermore, each participant in this process constituted suicide as a public action. The professionalization of suicidology in the twentieth century would remove these conversations from public view, and changes in taste and typography would reduce the amount of space given to suicide stories in twentieth-century newspapers, even in the "yellow press."[54] The argument could be made that the Victorian reader was more literate about their culture's thoughts on suicide, and more influential on their culture's thoughts on suicide, than any before or since. They responded with an appropriate sense of responsibility: after the report of a "touching case," police magistrates in London were "often inundated with earmarked donations."[55]

Teleological Suicides

Suicides were not uncommon in Victorian fiction, but they were often marginal, a means of resolving a narrative problem, explained in terms of the purposes they serve. The clearest iterations of this teleology of suicide are villains. Suicide is the

52 "SUICIDE OF A CHILD: DOCTOR'S DAUGHTER ENDS HER LIFE," *The Evening Telegraph and Star*, August 7, 1897.

53 "SUICIDE CATCHERS," *The Falkirk Herald and Midland Counties Journal*, November 28, 1900.

54 Anderson, *Suicide in Victorian and Edwardian England*, 251–2.

55 Anderson, *Suicide in Victorian and Edwardian England*, 300.

just desserts of a life of wickedness, capital punishment for crimes committed as well as a confirmation of villainous character, since the heroic do not choose death. The causes are apparent and the effects, the affirmation of a moral order in the universe. Judas Iscariot is a clear precedent, but contemporary examples abound. In Wilkie Collins's *Armadale* (1864–6), Lydia Gwilt twice attempts to poison her husband's best friend, then kills herself with poison gas. Hardy's *Desperate Remedies* (1871) concludes with the murderous, illegitimate-born bigamist Aeneas Manston hanging himself. Anthony Trollope sentences three fraudulent financiers to suicide: Dobbs Broughton shoots himself in *The Last Chronicle of Barset* (1867–8), Augustus Melmotte drinks prussic acid in *The Way We Live Now* (1874–5), and in *The Prime Minister* (1875–6), Ferdinand Lopez steps in front of a train. A punishment "almost equivalent for a Trollope character," writes John Halperin.[56] Robert Louis Stevenson synonymizes self-destruction and villainy in "The Suicide Club" (1878), which has the president of the title organization acting as the antagonist in three detective stories. Stevenson's more enduring creation, Henry Jekyll, is found with a crushed phial in his hand, while another Gothic antihero, Dorian Gray, chooses death when he stabs the picture that sustains his youth. In Arthur Machen's *The Great God Pan* (1894), Helen Vaughan drives Londoners to commit suicide and, given the choice between the noose and the police, she chooses the noose.

Suicide could also serve as punishment for more ambiguous crimes, especially those of women who yield to their passions. Lady Dedlock, an unwed mother, learns her daughter is still alive and flees her home in shame at the end of Dickens's *Bleak House*. She is later found dead at her lover's grave. Rosanna Spearman, more misguided than malicious, falls in love outside her social class, withholds evidence in the belief this will protect the man she adores, and leaps from the cliffs of the Shivering Sand, impeding the investigation at the center of Collins's *The Moonstone* (1868). In Hardy's *The Return of the Native* (1878), Eustacia Vye does not answer the door when her mother-in-law knocks, afraid of being found with a former lover. In consequence, her mother-in-law dies, her husband finds out she is responsible, and she drowns herself in a stream. Tess Durbeyfield offers to do the same when she confesses her murder of Alec to Angel. Herminia Barton, another unwed mother, drinks prussic acid for the sake of her daughter's happiness in Grant Allen's *The Woman Who Did* (1895), and Harriet Brandt poisons herself after she causes the death of her husband

[56] John Halperin, *Trollope and Politics: A Study of the Pallisers and Others* (Macmillan, 1977), 45.

in Florence Marryat's *The Blood of the Vampire* (1897). In Emma Brooke's *A Superfluous Woman* (1894), Jessamine Halliday weds a blue-blooded playboy with tainted blood. Their daughter kills their son and then herself; Jessamine wills a miscarriage and then her own demise.

Dickens was especially fond of the device: Ralph Nickleby, Jonas Chuzzlewit, Mr. Merdle, and Bradley Headstone all kill themselves. Consider Ralph as a representative example. When he learns that the boy he "has persecuted and hunted down […] to death" is his son, he smashes a lamp, casting the room into darkness, and disappears before light is restored.[57] The action is a metaphorical rehearsal of his imminent death. To paraphrase Othello, he puts out the light, then puts out the light. On his way home, Ralph "slink[s] off like a thief," and a "black gloomy mass" follows him "like a shadowy funeral train" (802). He continues to look over his shoulder, "as though he were followed in imagination or reality by someone anxious to question or detain him." His thoughts, demeanor, and even the weather all assure the reader of his guilt and its attendant punishment. His decision is immediate and definitive: "Ralph makes one last Appointment—and keeps it" is the title of the next chapter in which he appears. *Appointment* suggests a business obligation rather than the "rash act," and the proceedings, despite one emotional outburst, are neither hurried nor demonstrative. Always fastidious in such matters, Ralph's suicide is a calculated and orderly affair. The criminal is taking the punishment into his own hands.

Ralph's decision to kill himself is inspired by his participation in the trial of a suicide. He passes a "poor, mean burial ground" and recalls one of its occupants, a man, long forgotten, who cut his throat (802). Ralph served as a juror at the trial, and "he conjured up a strong and vivid idea of the man himself, and how he looked, and what had led him to do it" (803). He remembers "the pale and trembling relatives who had told their tale upon the inquest—the shrieks of women—the silent dread of men—the consternation and disquiet—the victory achieved by that heap of clay, which, with one motion of its hand, had let out the life and made this stir among them" (805). For a man who finds pleasure in frustrating the lives of his enemies, the chaos of suicide makes for an alluring exit. Perhaps this is why Dickens refrains from disclosing critical details of the man and his death. The narrator and Ralph's free indirect discourse never let on about "how he looked, and what had led him to do it." We only read that the

[57] Charles Dickens, *Nicholas Nickleby*, ed. Paul Schlicke (Oxford University Press, 2009), 789. All subsequent references are noted parenthetically in the text.

subject is on Ralph's mind, and the pained speech of the loved ones is reduced to unintelligible sounds or mere silence, the words bare, almost naked, when separated by a series of em dashes.

Such particulars are irrelevant, since Ralph only wants to perpetuate bedlam. Once home, he sees the cloud through a window and hears a single bell ring. It tolls, of course, for him, and like the black mass, the bell appears to have conspired with nature in pushing the villain toward the noose. Ralph accepts the verdict. A messenger interrupts him, and he replies that he will be "ready to receive" visitors at "any hour" the following day (806). By then, he will have met his obligations to the public, and he would therefore be "ready to receive" Nicholas, the standard-bearer of that public. Ralph cries, "No bell or book for me! Throw me on a dunghill, and let me rot there, to infect the air!" (806). He rejects the thesis of Donne's poem, which is a variation on Aquinas: we are all members of a whole, and the death of one is the death of all. Instead, he uses his demise as an ultimate rejection of a cohesive social fabric, a final puff of pollution to contaminate the air. It is a failure. Ralph misreads "the figure he had raised that night" (805). He dies intestate, his relatives reject his estate, and his money is returned to the crown. There is no bedlam in his wake. The results are the same as a successful prosecution of *felo de se*. Dickens has endowed his villain with limited agency. Ralph is permitted to usurp the role of the hangman, but he is denied the chaotic consequences he desires. His purpose, his teleology, is to insist that crime, whether moral or legal, is succeeded by punishment. Trollope, employing the financial language of *The Way We Live Now*, calls this Melmotte's "last grand payment."[58] However, the chapter "Ralph makes one last Appointment—and keeps it" does not depict the second half of its title. The narrator skips ahead to the discovery of Ralph's corpse, hanging "in the very place to which the eyes of his son, a lonely desolate little creature, had so often been directed in childish terror" (807). Poetic justice meted out to a man who has terrorized more than one child and reassurance to the reader that such behavior does not evade punishment.

The suicide of Bertha Mason is not a punishment, but its function is likewise teleological: it enables the happy marriage of Jane Eyre and Edward Rochester. Bertha herself is a ghost. Her "mirthless" laughter, her "goblin ha! ha!" haunt the passages of Thornfield from the moment our narrator crosses its threshold, but

[58] Anthony Trollope, *The Way We Live Now*, ed. John Sutherland (Oxford University Press, 1999), ii, 342.

we do not read the name Bertha Antoinetta Mason until the end of Volume II of *Jane Eyre* (1847), almost halfway through the novel.[59] Charlotte Brontë does not use her suicide to evoke the sympathy of the reader or imagine the "lived experience" of madness and suicide but to grease the wheels of her narrative. Since Gilbert and Gubar, at least, "the specter of Bertha" has been read as "Jane's truest and darkest double," as "the ferocious secret self Jane has been trying to repress ever since her days at Gateshead."[60] Both are imprisoned for their failure to cede to authority, both are prone to "flaming rages," and the scenes in the red-room serve as a counterpoint to the madwoman's attic (362). When Aunt Reed is on her deathbed, she remembers that Jane "talked to me once like something mad, or like a fiend" (231). The next time the word appears in the text, it is Rochester who is speaking about Bertha following his aborted wedding: Jane must leave this "narrow stone hell, with its one real fiend" (300). Comparing the two, he calls Jane "my better self—my good angel," Bertha, his "hideous demon" (315). Before order can be restored, before the good angel can triumph, the hideous demon in all its manifestations has to be purged. Thornfield must be burned to the ground, Bertha must kill herself, and Jane must molt her unruly double. "I love you better now, when I can really be useful to you," she tells Rochester, "than I did in your state of proud independence, when you disdained every part but that of the giver and protector" (445).

Jane shadows Bertha in her steps toward suicide. While locked in the red-room, she considers various means of "escape," including "never eating or drinking more, and letting myself die" (15). Jane, a mostly dutiful Victorian, is soon horrified that she contemplated choosing death, even a passive one: "That certainly was a crime" (16). At this point in the novel, she has spent her entire life as a burden to others whose disappearance would only bring relief, yet by framing suicide as a legal rather than a moral issue—she uses the word *crime*, not *sin*—Jane, like Aquinas, understands it as an offense against society. When she begins to get a whiff of a mystery at Thornfield, she repeats the word, asking, "What crime was this, that lived incarnate in this sequestered mansion, and could neither be expelled nor subdued by the owner?" (210) *Lived incarnate* indicates that Bertha is the personification of a crime, and by

[59] Charlotte Brontë, *Jane Eyre*, ed. Sally Shuttleworth (Oxford University Press, 2008), 107, 208. All subsequent references are noted parenthetically in the text.

[60] Sandra M. Gilbert and Susan Gubar, *The Madwoman in the Attic: The Woman Writer and the Nineteenth-Century Imagination* (Yale University Press, 2000), 359–60.

nineteenth-century standards, her "savage face," her "lips [...] swelled and dark," and "bloodshot eyes" all invoke a criminality associated with the Creole of the English imagination (284). Her suicide is written on her body; it is the fulfillment of a fixed state of criminal madness, one determined by three generations of "idiots and maniacs" (292). It is the realization of her character that is legible from her first appearance in Jane's room. Jane, who is sympathetic, says "that unfortunate lady [...] cannot help being mad" (301). This distinction in character is what separates Bertha from the others. Rochester, too, stares down the barrel of a gun, but he "only entertained the intention for a moment; for not being insane, the crisis of exquisite and unalloyed despair which had originated the wish and design of self-destruction was past in a second" (308). In the stark divisions Brontë sketches, neither Jane nor Rochester falls into a class of people who commit suicide ("not being insane"). On the other hand, Bertha's end is contained in her beginning, her drunk, Creole mother just one in a series of cues to her fate. It is no surprise Jane compares her to "the foul German spectre—the Vampyre," a creature that is neither alive nor dead (284). Or that Rochester, though wrong, assures Mason, "when you get back to Spanish Town, you may think of her as dead and buried" (213). The whole novel seems to insist on Bertha's suicide before she gets there herself.

Bertha is not the only character who is so marked. Brontë also dispatches John Reed, the cousin who terrorizes young Jane, to self-destruction. At fourteen, his body is bloated like Bertha's: he is "large and stout for his age, with a dingy and unwholesome skin; thick lineaments in a spacious visage, heavy limbs and large extremities [...] with a dim and bleared eye and flabby cheeks" (9 and 10). Late in the novel, when Jane asks the family coachman about him, she hears that he "ruined his health and his estate [...] How he died, God knows!—they say he killed himself" (222). Jane reports to Rochester that "he ruined himself and half-ruined his family, and is supposed to have committed suicide" (223). *Supposed*, rather than registering doubt, indicates collective agreement, the easy legibility of such actions. Within only one page, Jane has excised the irresolute "God knows!" from her retelling. Cause and effect are explained in fifteen words. John looks like a sinner. John acts like a sinner. Ergo John commits suicide. So much for him.

Because such legibility resolves why one chooses death, its meaning is redirected to what that does means to others. In the now-voluminous criticism on

Bertha, she is described as an avatar,[61] a surrogate,[62] a sacrifice,[63] an education.[64] In other words, she is a symbol whose meaning is determined by the viewer. For Rochester, she is "the thing [...] the maniac up-stairs" (310 and 316). For Jane, she is at first the "mystery at Thornfield," an entertainment she is trying to nose her way into (165). Since Jane does not witness the jump, the suicide is related to us secondhand, from a stranger to both reader and protagonist, the host of a local inn:

> And then they called out to him that she was on the roof; where she was standing, waving her arms, above the battlements, and shouting out till they could hear her a mile off; I saw her and heard her with my own eyes [...] I witnessed, and several more witnessed Mr. Rochester, ascend through the skylight on to the roof: we heard him call "Bertha!" We saw him approach her; and then, ma'am, she yelled, and gave a spring, and the next minute she lay smashed on the pavement.
>
> (428)

The innkeeper emphasizes the act of witnessing the suicide almost as much as the suicide itself—its audience extends a mile, he exaggerates—and by the end of his telling, that witnessing has become a collective experience, one shared even through common senses: *we* saw him approach her. Rochester never fills in the gaps here, and his "Bertha!" remains our single glimpse at his response to the incident. Subsequent conversations with Jane are consumed by self-pity, sexual insecurity, and suspicion about her relationship with St. John. Still, his "Bertha!" is more than her unheard yell, and while the innkeeper describes the cause ("[she] gave a spring") and the effect ("the next minute she lay smashed on the pavement"), the fall itself, the moment she makes contact with the pavement, is not described. Having served her purpose, Bertha disappears. There is no mention of an inquest, for which Rochester would likely provide evidence. Brontë admitted she had "not sufficiently dwelt" on pity for Bertha, that she "erred in making *horror* too predominant."[65] Her horror is the horror she inspires in those

[61] Gilbert and Gubar, *The Madwoman in the Attic*, 359.

[62] Susan Lynn Meyer, *Imperialism at Home: Race and Victorian Women's Fiction* (University of Michigan Press, 1996), 77.

[63] Gayatri Chakravorty Spivak, "Three Women's Texts and a Critique of Imperialism," *Critical Inquiry* 12, no. 1 (1985), 251.

[64] Elisabeth Bronfen, *Over Her Dead Body: Death, Femininity, and the Aesthetic* (University of Michigan Press, 1992), 222.

[65] Charlotte Brontë, *The Letters of Charlotte Brontë Volume Two: 1848–1851*, ed. Margaret Smith (Oxford University Press, 2000), 3. Emphasis in original.

she encounters, not the horror she experiences. She is a metaphorical ghost who literally haunts her home, dashing around at night in the shadows. Unlike in conventional ghost stories, her message remains uncommunicated. The haunting ends rather than begins with her violent death. In committing suicide, Bertha is becoming the good wife, the sacrificial instrument St. John wanted in Jane.

The attempted suicide of Mirah Lapidoth in George Eliot's *Daniel Deronda* (1876) is no less essential to the trajectory of its novel. Oliver Lovesey writes, "Her narrative functions to bring Deronda into an understanding of his identity and to embody the sufferings of all English Jews."[66] Near the end of Book II, in a chapter titled "Meeting Streams," Deronda is drifting, both literally and metaphorically, on a late July evening. He is in a contemplative mood "perhaps more common in the young men of our day—that of questioning whether it were worth while to take part in the battle of the world" (144–5). After preventing Mirah from drowning herself, Deronda is thrust into such a world. Her Jewishness enables him to realize his own, effecting the personal transformation Eliot's novel demands. Catherine Belsey, summarizing the major moves of realist fiction, writes that its characters "all learn from experience, moving in the course of the narrative towards an enhanced awareness of themselves and the world," while "ignorance, misunderstanding and misrecognition generate a series of crises (episodes) which finally produce a new and more stable pattern of relationships (closure."[67] Such transformation, even such closure, is reserved for Deronda, but it is caused by Mirah's suicide attempt.

Before he first sees her, Deronda is identified by Jewish clothing and Ashkenazi features: "Rowing in his dark-blue shirt and skull-cap, his curls [were] closely clipped" (155). Looking at Mirah, he is touched by her "little woman's figure" and cries out, "Great God!" (156). In case we read this expression of faith as idiomatic, the narrator follows, "the words escaped Deronda in a tone so low and solemn that they seemed like a prayer become unconsciously vocal." His heroism brings out a latent religiosity, and contact with a Jewish woman has already aroused a vocal spirituality. The impression of "this forsaken girl" leads him to wonder, "perhaps my mother was like this one," and sustained contact with Mirah and her brother bears out the suspicion. Here is how the chapter ends: "Deronda felt himself growing older this evening and entering on a new phase in finding a life

[66] Oliver Lovesey, "The Other Woman in *Daniel Deronda*," *Studies in the Novel* 30, no. 4 (Winter 1998), 512.

[67] Catherine Belsey, "Re-reading the Great Tradition," in *Re-reading English*, ed. Peter Widdowson (Routledge, 2003), 123.

to which his own had come—perhaps as a rescue; but how to make sure that snatching from death was rescue?" (163). The ambiguous "perhaps as a rescue" suggests the encounter saves Deronda in addition to Mirah, that the substance of this encounter is the effect it has on his development. The suicide attempt generates this enhanced awareness. In Eliot's free indirect discourse, Deronda is the subject and a contributor to the prose. Mirah, who has not yet given her name, is a type, the "fellow-creature" who ignites this intellectual *aliyah*. His place in the battle is now assured.

Deronda's initial impressions, like the innkeeper's of Bertha's, comprise the most thorough account of Mirah's suicide attempt. For him, the encounter is a cacophony of artistic allusions, and Mirah is a reflection of his own thoughts and words. He finds ready collaboration in his narrator, and the chapter opens with a quotation from Tennyson—in part, "this is truth the poet sings[...]"—an announcement that conflates artistic rendering with truth (154). Furthermore, Deronda's hands are described as "long, flexible, firmly-grasping hands, such as Titian has painted in a picture where he wanted to show the combination of refinement with force," an image that prepares us for the force of his coming decisive action (155). When he first spots Mirah, Deronda has just abandoned the idea of becoming an author, "a vocation which is understood to turn foolish thinking into funds," and he has "no thought of an adventure in which his appearance was likely to play any part." He is singing Gioachino Rossini's *Otello* (1816), in fact, and reads this woman entirely through his private web of musical and literary references, in effect diverting his just-abandoned creative energy toward the real world: she is Desdemona brought to life, "a figure which might have been an impersonation of the misery he was unconsciously giving voice to" (156). Even though "her eyes were fixed on the river with a look of immovable, statue-like despair," he ignores the warning sign, decides to respect the "delicate beauty, picturesque lines and color of the image," and moves on (157). Why not, when the despair is immovable, set in stone? One does not interfere with the drama of a Titian. Instead, one speculates and reflects on its characters, its artistry.

Finding the scene picturesque, Deronda lingers at the "deepening stillness and darkening masses of tree and building between the double glow of the sky and the river [...] as if they had been an unfinished strain of music" (158). He thinks of "some oriental poet," who describes the sunset as "God's call to the little stars, who each answer, 'Here am I,'" an image of unity between God's creativity and nature's action that would appeal to a man who rows down a river and chooses to sing the lines of a fictional gondolier. However, until this scene, he has been unable to integrate his life with his art-infused worldview. In the previous chapter, we learn that "[h]aving read Shakespeare as well as a great deal of history, he could have talked with the wisdom of a bookish child about men who were born out of wedlock [...] But he had never brought such knowledge into any association with his own lot" (139). Thus distracted, Eliot requires a second sighting to rouse Deronda to action, and he stops Mirah from jumping into the river before extending the charity of his friendship with the Meyricks. Soon, he reverts to literary allusiveness. When he briefly worries about their reaction to housing a Jew, he assures himself that "this delicate, sorrowful image of womanhood," this "lovely Jewess" will be greeted like "Rebecca in 'Ivanhoe'" (163).

At every turn, fiction, opera, and painting set the terms of the scene and establish the grammar of their encounter. Despite the availability of artistic precedents, Deronda's attempt to infer a narrative—he fears "the wretched home and cruel friends he imagined her to be fleeing"—is unsuccessful (160). Yet Eliot and Mirah continue to accommodate his tendency to overdetermine his experience with artistic allusions. Mirah's first words to him, "I saw you before [...] nella miseria [in misery]," quote the song from *Otello* (159). "It was you, singing?" she continues, "Nessun maggior dolore [No more pain]." In her dreamy recollection of the suicide attempt, his web becomes a part of her experience, and Mirah concludes, "Dolore—miseria—I think those words are alive" (161). The fragments "in misery" and "no more pain" appear to echo the logic of suicide, but the novel that follows rejects Shakespeare's tragedy, and Deronda, Eliot's Desdemona, will soon hear that he, too, is a Moor.

What is lost in Deronda's perspective of Mirah's "project of suicide," and in her dreamy and adulterated recollection, is the meaning of the action to the one who attempted it. "Remaining unchanged herself," writes Ellen B. Rosenbaum, "she will be the catalyst for Deronda's future, initiating the complex and volatile reactions that constitute his plot without undergoing any comparable development."[68] Victorian culture encouraged communal construction of suicide narratives, and the result often shrouds the victims, silencing their voices by speaking on their behalf. Here, it is Deronda and his narrator who speak for Mirah. When she does explain her behavior, she relies on religious history: "I know our fathers

[68] Ellen B. Rosenbaum, "Women's Speech and the Roles of the Sexes in *Daniel Deronda*," *Texas Studies in Literature and Language* 31, no. 2 (Summer 1989), 242.

slew their children and then slew themselves, to keep their souls pure. I meant it so" (161). The suicides at Masada performed a function for the zealots: they conformed to the will of God. Their subjective experiences are, from a religious perspective, irrelevant. Mirah's attempted suicide likewise performs a function for Eliot: it precipitates Deronda's discovery of his Jewishness. Her subjectivity, her "lived experience," is irrelevant. The action is understood in terms of cause and effect. The meaning of her suicide attempt is its meaning for others.

Child Suicide and the Limits of Teleology

Father Time, the child who hangs his siblings and then himself in Hardy's *Jude the Obscure* (1894–5), is no different from the preceding examples. Like Mirah Lapidoth and Bertha Mason before him, his suicide resolves a problem: it reduces the number of hungry mouths in a household without money and liberates his parents to pursue their lives unhampered by the obligation of children. But the cost his deaths incur renders its teleological function untenable. Readers can accept the suicide of a villain, since it affirms their belief in punishment for moral transgressions. They can accept the off-stage suicide of a madwoman if it furnishes their heroine with a husband. They cannot accept the suicide of a child as the price for his parents' self-realization. Who cares about Jude's dreams of Christminster when three children are dead?

Despite the fact that he is a suicide who shatters Victorian norms—Sally Shuttleworth calls him a "direct assault [...] on our novel reading sensibilities where children customarily represent hope for the future, a promise of continuity and development"—Father Time's impending death is evident to the reader long before it actually happens.[69] Here biology is destiny, and Father Time is the culmination of generations of antisocial behavior. Consider his father. After "predestinate Jude" confronts Arabella about her feigned pregnancy, she counterattacks with the information that "your father ill-used your mother, and your father's sister ill-used her husband [...] All you Fawleys be a queer lot as husbands and wives."[70] Later, his great-aunt Drusilla confirms the diagnosis: "There's sommat in our blood that won't take kindly to the notion of being

[69] Sally Shuttleworth, *The Mind of the Child: Child Development in Literature, Science, and Medicine, 1830–1900* (Oxford University Press, 2010), 133.

[70] Thomas Hardy, *Jude the Obscure*, ed. Patricia Ingham (Oxford University Press, 2002), 39, 64. All subsequent references are noted parenthetically in the text.

bound to do what we do readily enough if not bound" (65). Drusilla is speaking about marriage, but following their separation, his "mother soon afterwards died—she drowned herself, in short" (64). Life, too, is something to which we are bound. On hearing this news, Jude immediately attempts to drown himself. Walking onto a

> large round pond [… he] put one foot on the edge of the ice, and then the other: it cracked under his weight; but this did not deter him. He ploughed his way inward to the centre, the ice making sharp noises as he went. When just about the middle he looked around him and gave a jump. The cracking repeated itself, but he did not go down. He jumped again, but the cracking had ceased.
>
> (65)

The simple, declarative sentences mimic the detached and methodological tone of scientific discourse. The narrator almost only describes Jude's actions, the literal steps he takes to die. At the end of his experiment, he concludes, "He was not a sufficiently dignified person for suicide. Peaceful death abhorred him as a subject, and would not take him." He is the object of the sentence.

Of course, it is the news of this hereditary relationship to suicide, not only the relationship itself, which prompts Jude's suicide attempt. Hardy constructs his character through his lineage as well as the public's understanding of that lineage, and this understanding is potentially fatal. Jude hears about the chronic domestic unhappiness and ill-treatment from a secondhand source, but it has an immediate and permanent effect on his character. Drusilla concludes her brief family history with a partial but tantalizing bit of information: on the road to Fenworth a "gibbet once stood […] not onconnected with our history. But let that be" (65). The crime for which their relative was executed is unnamed; suicide is not impossible. The public understanding of his history and character, combined with his own, orients Jude toward self-destruction, albeit a slow one, "suicide by inches."[71] Jude's ending, like Bertha's, is contained in his beginning. Both Brontë and Hardy draw clear lines of cause and effect, but Hardy's is a hazy vision, an amalgamation of incomplete sources. In Marygreen, it is the public narrative that sentences Jude to death. They are a chorus chanting *biological destiny*. Eventually, Jude agrees, as if the evidence has finally convinced him. His suicide attempt has an empirical quality to its reasoning. Though emotional in its effects, it is rational in its determination, and it enables us to read his hopes

[71] Karl Menninger quoted in Frank Giordano Jr., "*I'd Have My Life Unbe*": *Thomas Hardy's Self-destructive Characters* (University of Alabama Press, 1984), 36.

for his son ("What I couldn't accomplish in my own person perhaps I can carry out through him" [268]) with proper irony.

From his arrival in Aldbrickham, Father Time is wearing the noose around his neck—a "victim of spoiled heredity," writes Elaine Showalter.[72] When the reader first meets the "boy with an octogenarian face" (300), he moves in "a steady mechanical creep" (267). He "seemed mutely to say: 'All laughing comes from misapprehension. Rightly looked at there is no laughable thing under the sun'" (265–6). Later, he tries but fails to smile. Again, the suicide is written on his body, from the wizened visage to the "mechanical creep," which suggests the kind of degeneration associated with madness and suicide. Father Time, like Bertha, has long been considered "more of a symbolic figure than a real one,"[73] even "a major discursive breach with the conventions of nineteenth-century realism,"[74] his suicide "the most flagrant instance of Hardy's preparedness to sacrifice verisimilitude to his diagrammatic design."[75] He is a canary in the coal mine, another unfortunate whose death augurs "the coming universal wish not to live" (326). It is therefore appropriate he is denied even the barest of identifiers, a given name. His stepmother, Sue Bridehead, eschews a christening—"if I died in damnation, 'twould save the expense of a Christian funeral" (270)—and even when he is "formally turned into 'Jude,' the apt nickname stuck to him" (287). His identity to others is his identity to the novel. Even taking his father's name is too specific, too personal. Instead, he uses one better suited for a character in a Christian allegory, an old man with a scythe and an hourglass, there to remind the reader of the creeping approach of death. This makes him, in a sense, the Victorian suicide par excellence: a symbol, a plot device, but not an autonomous or psychologically realized subject.

The true scandal of the little boy's suicide is that the novel sustains its reasoning. The much-discussed note, "*Done because we are too meny*," has, on its own terms, an irrefutable logic (325; emphasis in original); it is as if the children of Ireland had suggested their own murders in "A Modest Proposal" (1729).

[72] Elaine Showalter, "Syphilis, Sexuality, and the Fiction of the Fin de Siècle," in *Sex, Politics, and Science in the Nineteenth-Century Novel*, ed. Ruth Bernard Yeazell (Johns Hopkins University Press, 1986), 108.

[73] Gordon K. Walker, "Father Time's Suicide Note in *Jude the Obscure*," *Nineteenth-Century Fiction* 22, no. 3 (1967), 299.

[74] Michael Hollington, "Story, History, Allegory: Some Ironies of *Jude the Obscure* from a Benjamin Perspective," in *Thomas Hardy and Contemporary Literary Studies*, ed. Tim Dolin and Peter Widdowson (Palgrave Macmillan, 2004), 114.

[75] Mary Jacobus, "Sue the Obscure," *Essays in Criticism* 25, no. 3 (1975), 320.

Father Time "seemed to have begun with the generals of life, and never to have concerned himself with the particulars [...] regarding his companions as if he saw their whole rounded lives rather than their immediate figures" (267 and 266). This is an academic, almost sociological position, with its attention to life cycles rather than the needs of the present moment. It is also what enables his violent home economics. When the family arrives in Christminster, they are denied lodging. Father Time asks a series of questions, and Sue is too tired to lie:

> "Father went away to give us children room, didn't he?"
> "Partly."
> "It would be better to be out o' the world than in it, wouldn't it?"
> "It would almost, dear."
> "'Tis because of us children, too, isn't it, that you can't get a good lodging."
> "Well—people do object to children sometimes."
>
> (322)

Father Time says children should be killed at birth, and Sue decides to be "honest and candid" and admits that she is pregnant (323). He storms into his bedroom, the adjoining closet, and cries, "If we children was gone there'd be no trouble at all!" (324). The reader witnesses both his gathering of evidence and his conclusion. There is no cause to expect anything but what follows: by mid-morning, he and his siblings are dead. For Father Time, this is a gift to his parents, the resolution of a conflict, a macabre variation of the teleological tradition observed by Eliot, Brontë, Dickens, and others. Father Time is an obliging Bertha Mason. Margaret Oliphant, a contemporary critic who had favorably reviewed *Tess of the D'Urbervilles* (1891), complained in *Blackwood's Magazine*, "Mr. Hardy knows, no doubt as everybody does, that the children are a most serious part of the question of the abolition of marriage. Is this the way in which he considers it would be resolved best?"[76] Her question is rhetorical, from her perspective damning, but Father Time, at least, has answered it in the affirmative. In his Spartan rendering, an author prone to effusive speech from his central characters indicts the narrative that would demand such a conclusion. Even Sue admits, "It was not unreasonable for him to die: it was part of his incurably sad nature" (328), her use of *unreasonable* denoting a sort of judiciousness, *nature* her reliance on popular hereditary science, as in Jude's "It was in his nature to do it. The doctor says[...]" (326).

[76] Margaret Oliphant, "The Anti-Marriage League," in *Thomas Hardy: The Critical Heritage*, ed. R. G. Cox (Routledge, 2005), 273.

All three children are buried in a "common grave" (330). Sue blames her conversation with Father Time for his actions, and she is right: these deaths are her fault. The logic is merciless. Neither Jude nor, I suspect, the reader actually blames Sue, but the narrator, who structures the scenes back-to-back, makes a case for incrimination. No wonder she appeals to teleology, reading the deaths in functional, narrative-churning terms: "They were sacrificed to teach me how to live!—their death was the first stage of my purification," she cries, "That's why they have not died in vain!" (351–2). For the Hardy of *Jude the Obscure*, such transformations are not redemptive; they are poisonous. Father Time fails to account for the emotional consequences of his actions, and rather than resolving a conflict, he compounds one. No one "learn[s] from experience" or "produce[s] a new and more stable pattern of relationships." The tone reflects the barren crops: the description of this "triplet of little corpses"—"the girl and the baby boy" hung on "hooks for hanging garments [...] by a piece of box-chord round each of their necks"—is thorough but clinical to the point of indifference (325). While looking at her husband's "'andsome corpse," Arabella chats with the Widow Edlin (396). She asks about Sue, and Edlin tells her she looks "[t]ired and miserable," but offers consolation nonetheless: "She said she had found peace!" (397). Arabella rejects the widow's typical Victorian resolution: "She may swear that on her knees to the holy cross upon her necklace till she's hoarse, but it won't be true [...] She's never found peace since she left his arms, and never will again till she's as he is now!" Her cynical reading casts the suicide of little Jude as an irrevocable rupture, one that reaps death, disunion, and perpetual irresolution. There are no marriages, no realizations of religious faith, no affirmations of a moral order. Arabella's stand is the last word on this or any other matter in the novel.

Thus, even as moral outrage subsided and the harshest punishments were abolished, the English continued to view suicide as a public event. Victorian discourse on the subject was porous, assembled from a range of disciplines—religion, the law, literature—much of it available to the amateur reader. Debates centered on the effects of suicide rather than its causes. Should the crown continue to seize their assets? Should their body be admitted into the churchyard? Should locomotives add a "suicide catcher" to prevent the inconvenience of a death on public transportation? Novelists tended to avoid the depiction of suicide, and suicidal characters were often peripheral, instruments in the plot rather than the substance of the narrative. Their deaths are teleological. At the end of the nineteenth century, the rational suicide of Father Time ("*Done because we are too meny*") likewise resolves a problem, it reduces the number of mouths to feed, but the consequences of child suicide render such teleological explanations untenable. They would lose much of their currency in the twentieth century.

2

The Last Word: Suicide Notes in *The Sorrows of Satan* and *Strange Case of Dr. Jekyll and Mr. Hyde*

To quote Janet Todd: "A suicide note is a strange document."[1] Written in private about events and feelings that are also private, a suicide note is addressed to multiple audiences—family, loved ones, police, coroner, newspaper readers—and is therefore public, too. Michael MacDonald and Terence R. Murphy, discussing eighteenth-century notes, argue that their authors used them as "a means of perpetuating their identities beyond death, a literary substitute for speech and gesture, a last act of self-fashioning."[2] Because the note is written by the perpetrator, the reader will often treat its contents as authoritative, enabling the suicide to assert control over the reception of their death. Still, its authority is derived not from its contents but from what follows. A suicide note is a promissory note, and it has far less power if it is not soon vindicated by action. It requires the closure of death to ensure its hold over the narrative. For nineteenth-century readers, these notes provided insight into an action that remained a sin and a crime despite an increase in sympathy for the victims and the abolition of the most punitive laws. For suicides, they offered redemption through "a sentimental transaction between the dead author and the living reader."[3] The reader, after all, has the power to render the final verdict. The voices of the dead can be persuasive.

1 Janet Todd, "Suicide and Biography," *Comparative Criticism* 25 (2004), 59.

2 Michael MacDonald and Terence R. Murphy, *Sleepless Souls: Suicide in Early Modern England* (Clarendon Press, 1990), 334.

3 Eric Parisot, "Suicide Notes and Popular Sensibility in the Eighteenth-Century British Press," *Eighteenth-Century Studies* 47, no. 3 (Spring 2014), 284.

Suicide notes were rare in England before the eighteenth century, but they were "well established as a literary subgenre" by the 1770s.[4] Their purposes are manifold. Eric Parisot writes, "Some wrote to seek forgiveness, others to justify their actions. Some used their final opportunity to reiterate their devotion, while others chose to air the marital grievances that had driven them to breaking point, and to apportion blame."[5] Some notes doubled as a last will and testament, including instructions for the disbursement of property.[6] Ella Sbaraini documents a series of cases in which suicides employed a variety of materials in lieu of paper: the cell walls of a jail (1849), the shutters in a workshop (1783), and several rooms of an abandoned tenement—attic, staircase, and a lower room, all marked in black-lead pencil (1797).[7] There is some evidence to suggest that suicide notes increased the risk of their authors being ruled *felo de se*, since they could be used as evidence of sound mind.[8] On the other hand, there is the case of Emma Austin, who in 1862 was ruled *non compos mentis* because she left a poem for her husband, this evidence "of a romantic tendency."[9] The genre of her note, poetry, protected her from punishment. Nevertheless, suicide notes were and are uncommon.[10]

In England, newspapers published suicide notes, in contrast to France, where the government forbade the gazettes from even mentioning the subject.[11] These notes were genuine as well as counterfeit and sometimes published at the request of the suicide.[12] Since "postage was costly in this period," writes Sbaraini, "this allowed poorer people's letters to reach loved ones for free."[13] Take as an example one attributed to Mary Ann Tenant, who wrote to her cousin before drowning herself, "I did not want my brother John to go with Mary, and they knocked me down, and kicked me black and blue. Her mother and Julia and John turned

[4] MacDonald and Murphy, *Sleepless Souls*, 228, 326.

[5] Parisot, "Suicide Notes and Popular Sensibility," 280.

[6] MacDonald and Murphy, *Sleepless Souls*, 327–8; Victor Bailey, *"This Rash Act": Suicide Across the Life Cycle in the Victorian City* (Stanford University Press, 1998), 57; Ella Sbaraini, "The Materiality of English Suicide Letters, c.1700–c.1850," *The Historical Journal* 65 (2022), 632.

[7] Sbaraini, "The Materiality of English Suicide Letters," 622, 623.

[8] Parisot, "Suicide Notes and Popular Sensibility," 283–4; Sbaraini, "The Materiality of English Suicide Letters," 636–7.

[9] Olive Anderson, *Suicide in Victorian and Edwardian England* (Clarendon Press, 1987), 142.

[10] MacDonald and Murphy, *Sleepless Souls*, 229; Sbaraini, "The Materiality of English Suicide Letters," 617; Bailey, *This Rash Act*, 31.

[11] Georges Minois, *History of Suicide: Voluntary Death in Western Culture*, trans. Lydia G. Cochrane (Johns Hopkins University Press, 1999), 287.

[12] MacDonald and Murphy, *Sleepless Souls*, 316; Minois, *History of Suicide*, 294.

[13] Sbaraini, "The Materiality of English Suicide Letters," 621.

against me."[14] Clearly, this rebuke is meant to pain her living relatives, as it blames them for her death, but the expository "my brother" implies additional readers who need to be informed of the relationship between the characters in the drama. Others were more philosophical. The insurance collector Frank Howell announced from the pages of the *Cardiff Times and South Wales Weekly News*, "I long to solve the mysteries of eternity. I shall soon know what comes after death."[15] Following his sister's suicide and before his own, the electrician Edgar Herbert Dell addresses his note to his coroner, and all three hundred seventy-two words were printed in *The Yorkshire Evening Post*. The peroration reads:

> Enough! The history of the world cannot be written on a sheet of foolscap. Do you ask why men kill themselves? Then ask why, as one falls, why men mourn for the dead; why a north pole attracts a south; why a man loves a woman; and why men live. If you must have something other than unsound mind, let the verdict be death from inability to cope with the problems of life.[16]

Suicides who could not produce their own words found other means of self-expression, and some used "whole phrases" they read in the press.[17] John William Storey, a sailor who deserted from the Royal Navy, shot himself in 1898. In his pocket, he left a photograph of a young woman and the text of Hamlet's "To be or not to be."[18]

Contagion was a major concern of reformers, who routinely blamed the newspapers for the suicides they reported.[19] The nineteenth-century epidemiologist J. Netten Radcliffe called for the press to "declare a war to the knife [...] against all maudlin sentiment" on the subject.[20] William Farr, a leading medical statistician, insisted on "discontinuing, by common consent, the detailed dramatic tales of murder, suicide, and bloodshed in the newspapers."[21] Suicide notes were of particular concern, but public interest was not aligned with the morality of the reformers. In 1839, when twenty-three-year-old Margaret Moyes

[14] "A SUICIDE'S EXTRAORDINARY LETTER," *The Swindon Advertiser*, April 27, 1895.

[15] "A SUICIDE'S LETTER," *Cardiff Times and South Wales Weekly News*, July 15, 1893.

[16] "A SUICIDE'S LETTER TO THE CORONER: EXTRAORDINARY EPISTLE," *The Yorkshire Evening Post*, August 20, 1891.

[17] Minois, *History of Suicide*, 287.

[18] "THE SAILOR SUICIDE AND SHAKESPEARE," *The Evening Telegraph*, February 3, 1898.

[19] Anderson, *Suicide in Victorian and Edwardian England*, 374.

[20] Quoted in Anderson, *Suicide in Victorian and Edwardian England*, 352.

[21] Quoted in Barbara T. Gates, *Victorian Suicide: Mad Crimes and Sad Histories* (Princeton University Press, 1988), 42.

leapt from the Monument to the Great Fire of London, the scene was "crammed with people trying to gain access."[22] A little over a year later, fifteen-year-old Richard Hawes, a reader of murder stories, recreated Moyes's death after being fired from his job for threatening to jump out a window.[23] His Bible, left in the gallery with several pages turned down, "was read as a kind of suicide note."[24] An iron cage was finally installed on the Monument in 1842 after Jane Cooper, a servant, threw herself from the gallery, the sixth such suicide in the previous fifty-four years. In 1928, the establishment of the London Metropolitan Police Service brought suicide prevention—a form of infection control—under the purview of Scotland Yard. The new police undertook "regular patrolling" and were "constantly rescuing the local prostitutes" from the water under one bridge, nicknamed Mr. Baker's Trap for the coroner, William Baker, who would collect fees from their deaths.[25] Faced with a suicide, it became common in the second half of the 1800s for Londoners to call for a policeman.[26] "In the metropolitan area," writes Olive Anderson, "the primary role of the law in suicide prevention proves to have been not to punish, but rather to promote public order."[27]

As discussed in the previous chapter, suicide was a common fate for fictional villains, the action a confirmation of and punishment for their villainy. Charles Dickens comes close to representing Andrew Bennett's "phenomenology" or "lived experience [...] of suicide" in his depiction of Ralph Nickleby, but he, like most of his contemporaries, skips over the death to the discovery of the corpse.[28] In Wilkie Collins's *Armadale* (1864–6), Lydia Gwilt does leave a 168-word suicide note that the narrator quotes in full, but her death occurs behind a closed door: "Then, a sound came dull and sudden, like the sound of a fall."[29] At the end of the century, Marie Corelli and Robert Louis Stevenson would use the "well established [...] literary subgenre" of the suicide note to explore, in much greater depth, the voices of suicidal characters up to the moment of self-destruction. In the following chapter, I will argue that the suicide notes in *The Sorrows of Satan* (1895) and *Strange Case of Dr. Jekyll and Mr. Hyde* (1886) give readers an over-the-shoulder view of an action that is not quite villainous and not quite good.

[22] Gates, *Victorian Suicide*, 39.
[23] Gates, *Victorian Suicide*, 43.
[24] Gates, *Victorian Suicide*, 44.
[25] Anderson, *Suicide in Victorian and Edwardian England*, 355 and 356.
[26] Anderson, *Suicide in Victorian and Edwardian England*, 377.
[27] Anderson, *Suicide in Victorian and Edwardian England*, 423.
[28] Andrew Bennett, *Suicide Century: Literature and Suicide from James Joyce to David Foster Wallace* (Cambridge University Press, 2017), 4.
[29] Wilkie Collins, *Armadale*, ed. Catherine Peters (Oxford University Press, 2009), 807.

Because it is not quite villainous, the reader can sympathize. Because it is not quite good, we require fiction as a moral intermediary. Only through a border character, like a villain, is this possible; it creates a window of permissiveness. The novel, more respectable and responsible than the yellow press, serves as a kind of moral prophylactic, enabling exposure to suicidal thoughts without risk of repeating them.

The Sorrows of Satan

Corelli's *The Sorrows of Satan* is a Faustian satire with two targets. The first is the publishing industry, which Corelli charges with corruption. Editors are only interested in salacious material. Manuscript readers are authors themselves and are motivated to "foster mediocrities and suppress originality."[30] Reviewers are considered "smart" when they abuse books they have not read. The novelist who writes about "the noblest forms of life" will be met with suggestions such as "Put in as much as you can about sexual matters" (29). And everyone can be bought. When Corelli writes, "for forty pounds, a well-known 'agency' will guarantee the insertion of *any* paragraph, provided it is not libelous, in no less than four hundred newspapers," the sum "forty pounds" is footnoted with two words: "A fact" (59; emphasis in original). Still, the practice of "booming" produces fame but not readers, and a masterpiece cannot be written in an environment of luxury. The only means of achieving true success is through honest labor and the affection of the public. Corelli's second target is the "fashionable folks," those arbiters of taste who have abandoned religious faith with modish indifference. An early and typical sentence includes the parenthetical remark, "([...]some belated folk still fancy there is a God somewhere)" (20). In this milieu, belief is an anachronism (*belated*), believers are misguided (*fancy*) and unsure (*somewhere*), and their faith is an afterthought (the parentheses). Under these conditions, Satan no longer commands the fear of the elite victims who constitute so much of his work, and his job has become perfunctory. Here is a melancholy Prince of Darkness, one who longs to return home but is condemned to tempt man into sin. Each success, he complains, is "another bar between myself and heaven" (94).

[30] Marie Corelli, *The Sorrows of Satan, or the Strange Experience of One Geoffrey Tempest, Millionaire: A Romance* (Oxford University Press, 1996), 6. All subsequent references are noted parenthetically in the text.

Corelli illustrates her arguments through, as her subtitle indicates, *The Strange Experience of One Geoffrey Tempest, Millionaire*. Tempest, our narrator, is the son of a landowner and a graduate of Oxford, but after his father's death, the creditors leave him with nothing but a jeweled miniature of his mother, who died in childbirth. He earns a living by hack work and fails to secure a publisher for his manuscript until the death of a distant relative leaves him with five million pounds. This unexpected inheritance coincides with an introduction to Lucio Rimânez, a beautiful, enigmatic, and cynical benefactor whose given name is one of a near-endless number of clues to his true identity. Rimânez guides Tempest through the purchase of literary and social success, facilitating the publication and enthusiastic reception of his manuscript as well as his marriage to Lady Sibyl Elton, the daughter of an impoverished earl. Sibyl is a student of the "new" fiction, so she feels nothing and speaks without embarrassment of the transactional nature of their engagement. After their wedding, she tells her husband, "My dutiful desire is to give you as much full value as I can for your money" (249). Tempest ignores these warning signs, but when he overhears Sibyl professing her love to Rimânez—and begging him for sex—he leaves her, and she swallows poison. Tempest considers suicide, too, but he is redeemed by a divine vision and the friendship of Mavis Clare, a middle-class novelist who shares the Christian values and the initials of her author. Corelli's use of the word *one* in the title implies Tempest, like Thomas Hood's Unfortunate, is a kind of case study that could be replicated across the urban centers of England.

Suicide follows Rimânez—a common fate of those who deal with the devil, as voluntary death is a rejection of God's ownership over our bodies. During a game of baccarat, Rimânez challenges Viscount Lynton, a reckless gambler, to stake his soul. Since no one present believes in the soul, Lynton accepts. His loss is followed by "the loud report of a pistol" from his hansom (91). Tempest agonizes over the death, but Rimânez is glib: "I told you he was a good shot!" (97). Rimânez predicts the ruling will be temporary insanity, as the "coroner's verdict always disposes of these incidents comfortably in two words" (92). The following morning, the papers do report the death, as well as the conveyance of the corpse to the mortuary to await an inquest, but apart from some allusions to money difficulties, "there was nothing said, either personal or particular" (97). *The Sorrows of Satan* bears out Rimânez. Lynton is so unimportant to its characters and its narrative that this "nothing said" is the last we hear of him. His death does not matter. The results of the inquest, it seems, are a foregone conclusion. The final word comes from Lord Elton: "Bad taste—bad taste! spoiling a poor cabby's stock-in-trade to satisfy a selfish whim!" (109).

Lynton is not written as a villain, so his suicide doesn't function to punish him for his crimes, as it does with Ralph Nickleby or Lydia Gwilt. That would be cruel. Like Hood's "The Bridge of Sighs," this is not an indictment of character but an indictment of the culture that has formed that character. Corelli uses Lynton's suicide as evidence to support her accusation of religious and moral decline. When Lynton leaves the club, its other members discuss his ruin "indifferently, as though one should talk of the weather—no sympathy was expressed, no pity wasted" (90). *Wasted* indicates there is a finite supply of pity that should be spent judiciously. (The economy of the "two words," temporary insanity, does the same.) When Rimânez says the verdict *comfortably disposes* of the matter, *disposes* makes the dead trash to be rid of, while *comfortably* denotes comfort not for the loved ones but for those who cannot be bothered to apportion a thought or sentiment to the victim. For his part, Lord Elton is more concerned with capital than life. He seems to find suicide rude. The "loud report" from the hansom stands as the single point in time when all attention is directed toward Lynton. Moments later, almost everyone moves on. Postcards from a culture on the road to damnation. Rimânez mocks the euphemism *temporary insanity* because it "covers up his plunge into the infinite with an untruthful pleasantness" (92). What really "drive[s] the distracted human unit to make of himself also a nothing"—and he is speaking for his author here—are "remorse, despair, outraged honour, [and] wasted love, together with the scientific modern theory of Reasonable Nothingness—Life a Nothing, God a Nothing" (92). Lynton's acquaintances prefer untruthful pleasantness because it is less intrusive on their own lives. The consideration of remorse, despair, honor, and love would all demand more sympathy for the victim. There is simply not enough to spare. Rimânez says murders and suicides "happen every day [...] they are perfectly common-place" (127). Is one expected to waste pity each time? After all, you can't control the weather.

When Sibyl swallows poison, the argument is the same: a corrupt tree bears evil fruit. Sibyl is the product of her decadent environment, and she leaves a last testament as evidence. She writes her suicide note out of curiosity, to investigate "whether indeed I was born evil from the first," and she concludes she was not (323). Instead, her mind has been adulterated by the wrong kind of literature: "All the fashionable fiction of the day passed through my hands, much to my gradual enlightenment, if not to my edification" (324). Sibyl's relationship to this fiction is spiritual (*enlightenment*) rather than educational (*edification*); it has replaced what would have been—and, for Corelli, what should have been—her relationship to God. She charges Swinburne, in particular, with "carrying impure suggestion into minds that were once cleanly and simple" (325). In this metaphor, Swinburne's poetry is an infectious disease, its symptoms the distraction of the human mind. Sibyl even links him to the instrument of her death, writing, "I believe there are many women to whom his works have been deadlier than the deadliest poison" (325). She has made the comparison twice before (162 and 247), perhaps in imitation of her father, who made it first (116). Cause and effect are not in doubt. It is as if the poet has filled the flask himself.

Sibyl has no ethical objections to suicide, does not fear "the powers invisible" (335), and dies "in utter atheism, rejoicing that there is no God and no Hereafter!" (334). Her approach to death is cool. She begins, unceremoniously, "I have made up my mind to die" (319). She is not acting "out of passion or petulance" but is making a "deliberate choice," which she finds a "necessity," since her "body is tired of life" (319). Her claims of dispassion are vindicated by her tone. Phrases like "hence it comes that I must die" (333) and "it is best to make an end" (319) muster all the enthusiasm of someone who has found the solution to a mildly challenging puzzle. The only apparent emotion Sibyl experiences is at the prospect that death "will be at any rate a new sensation not without interest" (336). She anticipates sensual rather than religious experience, and she doesn't understand the moral implications of suicide. For Corelli, she represents the failures of "these 'new women' days" (164). The parable of Reasonable Nothingness.

The note also includes, rather preposterously, the sequel to Sibyl's suicide, a vision of hell that bares "the awful Truth [...] there is No death!" (338). There is "nothing in the Universe but life" (338). Death is "a mere human dream—a comforting fancy" (339). Sibyl's shaking hands are "the throes of birth" and twice she writes, "*I cannot die*" (338 and 339; emphasis in original). Her suicide note is a revelation, an account of divine encounter. Corelli even suggests it could be the composition of a higher power, as "the pen I try to hold writes of itself rather than through my shaking hand" (339). The fire-and-brimstone conclusion is a warning. Since there is life after death, suicide is impossible. The ostensible self-destruction launches the unrepentant sinner into damnation, not extinction. "Nothing can be entirely annihilated; not even a thought," Rimânez tells Tempest (47). The tragedy of suicide is not that it is the end, but that it is another beginning, and a beginning that will damn the soul. In opposition to the atheistic new fiction she satirizes, Corelli argues that life is something, that God and Satan exist, that what we do matters. A man cannot make of himself a nothing.

In his reception of the body, Tempest fails to glean this lesson. There is something alien about the final encounter between the couple. When he first enters Sibyl's bedroom, Tempest touches "something clammy and cold like dead flesh," and he recoils (314). He turns on the electric light, much like lifting a curtain, and he questions whether the "strange, stiff white creature" before him is really his wife (314). She is a "frozen statue of a woman," an "ivory goddess," and a "waxen model," all variations on a sculpture metaphor (315). When he touches her hand—"Cold as ice it lay in my palm" (315)—the scene reads like a reversal of *The Winter's Tale* (1611). She's cold. Rather than a moment of revelation, a lifting of the curtain, this reinforces the distance between the two. Tempest makes it clear he finds "her ladyship's rash act" insincere and affected (316). In his rendering, it is a parody of the melodramatic, "fashionable" death of the late nineteenth century. Five times, he calls her suicide note a "manuscript," associating it with his failed fiction (331, twice on 339, 343, and 346). He also uses the terms "last document" (319) and "dying speech" (332). Both in quotation marks, these sneering phrases construe the note as a last will and testament as well as a soliloquy—O happy dagger!—and Tempest treats it with cynicism. He excuses Mavis from the room by joking, "the last message from the beloved dead is sacred" (317). Standing before Sibyl's corpse, he apostrophizes, "I have heard that the dead can speak at times [...] Shall I read your petition for forgiveness here?" (317 and 318). The reading of the petition is pro forma. Even without his bias toward the petitioner, he is predisposed to an ungenerous ruling: three paragraphs into the novel, he writes that he endured the kicks and blows of authority because he "scorned the cowardice of self-destruction" (5).

After he reads Sibyl's note, Tempest reassesses the scene and thinks, "what a 'fashion-plate' she would make now [...] for a frivolous and hypocritical 'ladies' paper" (340). Earlier in the novel, Rimânez arranges for a presentation of a series of tableaux vivant to celebrate his benefactor's wedding. Each is a parody of the audience, and each time the audience fails to recognize the self-portrait. The penultimate tableau is titled "Seeds of Corruption," and it depicts a teenage girl surrounded by "sexual" novels, to which Sibyl replies, "That is a *true* picture!" (222 and 223; emphasis in original). With the scene of her death, Corelli restages this tableau. Tempest finds the corpse "staring at itself in the silver-framed mirror with wide-open, fixed and glassy eyes!" (314–15). On her toilet-table, there is "a small dark-coloured bottle labelled 'Poison'" (316). Around her waist, she wears Rimânez's wedding gift, "the flexible emerald snake with its diamond crest and ruby eyes" (318). The image is effective because it is legible: the heavy-handed allusion to the fall of man; the bottle helpfully labelled "Poison"; the ironic contrast of the silver frame; and the macabre spectacle of a Narcissus-like figure recoiling in horror at its own reflection. It could be the final illustration in one of William Hogarth's modern moral subjects.

Tempest comes to the same conclusion as Sibyl: her suicide is an illustration of her corruption. What he fails to see is that it is also an illustration of his. After reading the note, he stares "into the mirror which pictured us both, we 'twain in one,' as the sentimentalists aver of wedded folk, though in truth it often happens that there are no two creatures in the world more widely separated than husband and wife" (318). The reference to "The Gospel of Mark" misquotes the verse and eliminates the final word in each clause. In full, it reads, "And they twain shall be one flesh: so then they are no more twain, but one flesh" (10:8). The quotation marks suggest that Tempest believes he is citing scripture, but instead of writing *twain (or, two) become one*, he writes *twain in one*, a phrase that sounds more like the split identities of Jekyll and Hyde than it does marital unity. Tempest is attempting to distinguish himself from Sibyl so he can be absolved of responsibility for her death. As Jill Galvan writes, "his self-satisfaction prevents him from seeing either this ugliness or his own sinfulness."[31] He refuses to recognize that the mirror reflects him, too.

There is reason to believe that Corelli would like her readers to derive different conclusions than her narrator. When Tempest writes, "the dead can speak at times," the character is sarcastic, but his author is sincere. For Corelli, the last message of the dead is sacred, and we should listen. It is this failure to sympathize that defines Tempest's marriage to Sibyl—in her note, she writes, "If he had studied my nature, entered into my emotions, or striven in the least to guide and sustain me [...] I think I should be sorry for him now" (319). This first-person account of suicide gives us the knowledge that Tempest never cared to learn: Sibyl was fallen and in need of salvation. Instead, he asks Mavis to take a look, since "part of the profession of literature is the ability to skim books and

[31] Jill Galvan, "Corelli's Caliban in a Glass: Realism, Antirealism, and *The Sorrows of Satan*," *English Literature in Transition, 1880–1920* 57, no. 3 (2014), 349.

manuscripts rapidly, and grasp the whole gist of them in a few minutes" (343–4). He fails to see the masterpiece in the slush.

The note is not only a cautionary tale but also an extended rebuttal to the "nothing said" that followed Lynton's suicide. With Lynton, Corelli builds an indictment on the indifference of his peers. With Sibyl, she appeals to the sympathy of the reader. Like printed stories of suicide, this is an opportunity "for the reader to test their own capacity to feel and, should the chance arise, to provoke substantive moral response beyond the gift of a tear."[32] The note comprises two chapters, nineteen section breaks, and almost ten thousand words, longer than this chapter. The size and weight alone make it resistant to quick characterization or dismissal. Even if Tempest has played editor, as the ellipses indicate, this is a remarkable attempt to imagine the experience of voluntary death. The reader, unlike the narrator, studies Sibyl's nature and enters into her emotions, and this is a perspective that is rare in English fiction for its scope and sympathy. We are not quite "one flesh," but we are, through the act of reading, an approximation of one mind. This is not free indirect discourse. It is discourse. R. Brandon Kershner calls it "suicide in slow motion," and the effect of slow motion is to provide the reader with the time to sympathize with Sibyl beyond the ready clichés about fallen women.[33] Its purpose is ethical, to discourage suicide and to convert those who do not care. If Corelli believed she could persuade impressionable youth to avoid new fiction and its consequences, she may have been right: after the publication of her first novel, *A Romance of Two Worlds* (1886), she received letters from readers claiming it was responsible for "conversions and salvation from suicide."[34] Sibyl's death is teleological even beyond the bounds of the narrative. Corelli writes to save her readers' souls, to "immunize [them …] from corruption."[35] She produces a suicide note that is both a critical memoir and a transcription of death and damnation. Since Sibyl is not born evil, since she occupies the middle ground between villain and not-villain, we can allow ourselves to sympathize with her circumstances. Since we are vulnerable to the effects of new fiction, we can assure ourselves that this over-the-shoulder look is inoculation, not prurience. Or worse—contamination.

[32] Parisot, "Suicide Notes and Popular Sensibility," 279.

[33] R. Brandon Kershner, "Corelli's Religious Trilogy: *Barabbas*, *The Sorrows of Satan*, and *The Master-Christian*," in *A Companion to Sensation Fiction*, ed. Pamela K. Gilbert (Wiley-Blackwell, 2011), 600.

[34] Christiane Gannon, "Marie Corelli's *The Sorrows of Satan*: Literary Professionalism and the Female Author as Priest," *English Literature in Transition, 1880–1920* 56, no. 3 (2013), 379.

[35] Simon J. James, "Marie Corelli and the Value of Literary Self-Consciousness: *The Sorrows of Satan*, Popular Fiction, and *Fin-de-Siècle* Canon," *Journal of Victorian Culture* 18, no. 1 (2013), 143.

Strange Case of Dr. Jekyll and Mr. Hyde

Over-the-shoulder is the default position of the reader throughout *Strange Case of Dr. Jekyll and Mr. Hyde*. Our surrogate is Utterson, "the dry lawyer," well-liked after dinners because his "silent" and "unobtrusive" company allows his interlocutors to "practic[e] for solitude, sobering their minds in the man's rich silence after the expense and strain of gaiety."[36] Ascetic and free of character, Utterson is likewise unobtrusive to the reader. His emptiness enables us to slip into his skin, and we get to "be Mr. Seek," too (15). Perhaps there is no better proof of Utterson's transparency than his disappearance from most major adaptations of the novella.[37] He is present in every scene of Stevenson's *Strange Case*, but he is inconsequential to the story and its afterlives because he exists only as our portal into the drama. In other media, he can be replaced by a camera, a microphone, or an illustrator's pen. Some critics have found more depth in the lawyer. Masao Miyoshi points to his indifference to the death of Sir Danvers Carew and argues that his tolerance for misbehavior has "the subtlest suggestion of vicarious pleasure."[38] Elaine Showalter reads his "self-mortification" as a means to "keep down" his "unconventional side [...] an effort to stay within the boundaries of masculine propriety."[39] I take both points but would venture that we are far too concerned with our own vicarious pleasure to be bothered with subtle suggestions from our tour guide. There are more urgent mysteries than the heart of Gabriel John Utterson, and his eccentricities do little to interfere with our identification with his point of view. Our quarry is Edward Hyde. Henry Jekyll calls him his "vicarious depravity," and Stevenson's narrative is structured around the deferral and ultimate satisfaction of this depraved pleasure (18). The reader is following Utterson, who is following Jekyll, who is following Hyde. Each is deriving satisfaction from the behavior of the person ahead of them.

[36] Robert Louis Stevenson, *Strange Case of Dr. Jekyll and Mr. Hyde*, ed. Katherine Linehan (Norton, 2003), 19. All subsequent references are noted parenthetically in the text.

[37] He is a main character in the first three stage versions—by Thomas Russell Sullivan (1887), John McKinney (1888), and Luella Forepaugh and George F. Fish (1897)—as well as the 1990 musical. He has a minor role in George Edwards' 1932 radio production, where he is upstaged by his daughter, Margaret. On film, he has more or less vanished. He has an uncredited role in the 1920 and 1931 Paramount movies, but he is absent from the 1941 MGM movie as well as all three Hammer adaptations, *The Ugly Duckling* (1959), *The Two Faces of Dr. Jekyll* (1960), and *Dr. Jekyll and Sister Hyde* (1971). In *Mary Reilly* (1996), his dramatic function is assumed by the title domestic.

[38] Masao Miyoshi, "Dr. Jekyll and the Emergence of Mr. Hyde," *College English* 27, no. 6 (March 1966), 471.

[39] Elaine Showalter, "Dr. Jekyll's Closet," in *The Haunted Mind: The Supernatural in Victorian Literature*, ed. Elton E. Smith and Robert Haas (Lanham, 1999), 71.

Our vantage point is privileged. To achieve his effects, Stevenson relies on the accumulation of evidence, which gives the reader the sense of being there, of overhearing private conversations and handling confidential documents. We are among the few granted access to this mystery, as the story unfolds in a fog of English restraint. When Utterson asks Enfield if he inquired further about "the place with the door," where Enfield saw Hyde retrieve a check, his reply summarizes the attitude of the book: "No, sir: I had a delicacy [...] I feel very strongly about putting questions" (11). All of them have a delicacy. So we begin at a distance, in a story within a story that alludes to but does not name the doctor. That does not happen until chapter 2, and Jekyll himself does not appear until Chapter 3, no short absence considering the length of the book. Still, there is no scarcity of breadcrumbs. In addition to the title, five of the ten chapters refer to documentary evidence: *story* (Chapter 1), *case* (4 and 10), *letter* (5), *narrative* (9), and *statement* (10). All of these require unwrapping. When Dr. Hastie Lanyon dies, he leaves an envelope marked "PRIVATE," and inside, there is an "enclosure," not to be opened until the death of Jekyll (30). Following that death, Jekyll bequeaths his own envelope, this one with three enclosures: a revised will, a short note, and a "confession" (41). Stevenson's title, *Strange Case*, puns on this, as *case* can be a verb meaning "to enclose, encase; to put in a case" (OED). The reader is present when each piece of evidence is removed from its case. Our view is not omniscient, but we do feel in at the death.

Above all evidence, Stevenson prizes handwriting. There is the "murderer's autograph" (28), the "holograph" will (12), the pious work "annotated, in [Jekyll's] own hand, with startling blasphemies" (40). It even reaches the level of metaphor: when Utterson first meets Hyde, he swears, "if ever I read Satan's signature upon a face, it is on that of your new friend" (17). The Miltonian sibilance links *Satan* with *signature*, as if the first were embedded in the second. For Stevenson, handwriting is an intellectual and a material expression of character. Both the style of the script and the substance of the words reflect the writer's mind. Gordon Hirsch challenges the evidentiary value of handwriting—because the pair "can write in either hand," it fails "to be distinctive, unique, proof of identity"—yet this is precisely what makes it all three: Jekyll and Hyde are not two but one.[40] They are separate choices made by the same personality, and the slopes that differentiate the handwriting of one from the other represent

[40] Gordon Hirsch, "Frankenstein, Detective Fiction, and Jekyll and Hyde," in *Dr. Jekyll and Mr. Hyde After One Hundred Years*, ed. William Veeder and Gordon Hirsch (University of Chicago Press, 1988), 238.

those choices. Hyde can play Jekyll just as Jekyll can play Hyde. It is Jekyll, after all, who "supplied my double with a signature" (53). This is his "own hand backward," *backward* a clue to the antisocial nature of the choice. Their handwriting is metaphorically legible as well as "distinctive, unique, proof of identity." When Jekyll writes that his is the "one part" of his "original character" that remains while he is "in my second character," Stevenson is punning on the overlap between character and character (52).

The novella culminates in its final, unabridged piece of evidence, a handwritten apology and suicide note. Jekyll describes the document as a *confession*, which indicates a desire for redemption, even if the note fails to fulfill its three traditional components (contrition, confession, and satisfaction). Stevenson, in his chapter title, uses the term *statement*, with connotations more legal than religious. Sinners confess, witnesses give statements. Under this double characterization, Jekyll is throwing himself on the mercy of both God and the court, a jury of readers. Neither word is wrong; both are incomplete. This is a cradle-to-grave memoir, perhaps better suited for *narrative*, with its implications of closure, which Stevenson uses for the previous chapter. As if to account for this inadequacy, all three words (*confession*, *statement*, and *narrative*) are used in the final paragraph (61–2). This version of events does not answer every question raised by the text, but it does attempt to explain how a Henry Jekyll could unleash an Edward Hyde. It is a first-person etiology of self-destruction.

The deaths of both Jekyll and Hyde conform to the teleological conventions of fictional Victorian suicide. They are guilty of assault and murder, as well as tinkering with the mechanics of man, and must be punished for their crimes. In a story defined by mystery, this is one plot point that should come as no surprise. Like Bertha Mason, with her "bloodshot eyes" and her "lips [...] swelled and dark," Hyde is marked for death.[41] In addition to the face inscribed with Satan's signature, he is, according to witnesses, "troglodytic" (17, Utterson), "deformed" (11, Enfield), and "ape-like" (21, the narrator; 61 and 62, Jekyll). The scene of the crime is unambiguous. Utterson knows "by the crushed phial in the hand and the strong smell of kernels that hung upon the air [...] that he was looking on the body of a self-destroyer" (39). Not just *a self-destroyer*, but *the body of a self-destroyer*—the evidence is in the flesh. Critics have long remarked that these descriptions are consistent with contemporary theories of degeneration, and removing Hyde from the gene pool would serve a perceived eugenic good.

[41] Charlotte Brontë, *Jane Eyre*, ed. Sally Shuttleworth (Oxford University Press, 2008), 284.

In his landmark study *Suicide and Insanity* (1893), the physician and barrister S. A. K. Strahan argues, "In some cases the suicide does society little, if any, injury, and in others he actually confers a favour upon it by quitting it." Sometimes, he writes, "suicide is a gainer."[42] The novella's opening anecdote, with its overtones of pedophilia, hints at what Hyde might spawn in both psychological damage and biological offspring. The suicide is teleological because it protects London from further violence and saves the reader from Hyde and everything he allegorizes. Its purpose is to render a verdict and to uphold the values of the culture they violated. A contemporary reviewer for the *Birmingham Daily Post* writes that Hyde "has yet enough of common sense to commit suicide."[43] The tone is approving.

But is Hyde responsible for their suicide? Critics have declined to answer this question with conviction. Andrew Smith argues that "the ending [is] radically open, as we cannot be sure if Jekyll kills Hyde [...] or if Hyde kills Jekyll."[44] Hirsch volunteers the noncommittal, "Probably the short answer is Hyde."[45] The popular imagination seems to concur, as the few adaptations that include the suicide—the first three stage versions, the 1912 Thanhouser Company film, *Mary Reilly* (1996)—attribute it to Hyde. The evidence suggests otherwise. The statement includes the line, "That night I had come to the fatal cross roads," a reference to the internment of suicides (51). Moreover, cyanide points to Jekyll. Suicides tend to use familiar objects, and the broken phial is an instrument from a professional life, not a debauched one. Wouldn't Hyde be more likely to choose a scalpel or a surgical knife? When Utterson offers help to Jekyll, the doctor insists that "the moment I choose, I can be rid of Mr. Hyde" (20). The remainder of the narrative belies his confidence, but it is a claim he reiterates in his statement: he has the "power to cut him off by suicide," a power he holds because Hyde has a "love of life" and a "fear of death" (61). The reader is denied Hyde's account of events, but it is difficult to imagine he would contest the characterization. Under the somewhat-puritanical terms of both Jekyll and Stevenson, an overflow of life must be stemmed, even by means of death. Death is the ultimate form of repression.

42 S. A. K. Strahan, *Suicide and Insanity* (Swan Sonnenschein, and Co., 1893), 219.

43 Quoted in Katherine Lineham, ed., *Strange Case of Dr. Jekyll and Mr. Hyde*, ed. Robert Louis Stevenson (Norton, 2003), 94.

44 Andrew Smith, "'The Body of a Self-Destroyer': Suicide and the Self in the *Fin-de-Siècle* Gothic," in *Suicide and the Gothic*, ed. William Hughes and Andrew Smith (Manchester University Press, 2019), 71.

45 Hirsch, "Frankenstein, Detective Fiction, and Jekyll and Hyde," 236.

For Jekyll, the suicide is also an ironic form of self-preservation. The note gives him the opportunity to have his confession heard, and his death protects the note: "Should the throes of change take me in the act of writing it, Hyde will tear it in pieces" (61). He destroys the body to preserve the mind—or, if you would rather, the soul. The suicide also gives him the last word, both literal and figurative. Because it covers his entire life, the statement feels complete, and because it feels complete, it reads as authoritative. This authority is derived from his subsequent and immediate death. When Jekyll calls its conclusion "my true hour of death, and what is to follow concerns another man than myself," he is insisting on that authority, despite knowing that he might once again be overcome by the throes of change (62). Jekyll believes that *conclusion* and *resolution* are synonymous. When he appeals to Lanyon for help, he uses the Psalmist phrase "my troubles will roll away like a story that is told" (43). The final line of the novella connects his death to the completion of the statement: "Here then, as I lay down the pen and proceed to seal up my confession, I bring the life of that unhappy Henry Jekyll to an end" (62). Stevenson phrases the sentence so that it can be read as causal (i.e., *because I lay down my pen, I bring my life to an end*). The suicide ensures that both Jekyll and his *Strange Case* end simultaneously.

Blaming Hyde for the suicide is an understandable reflex after centuries of villainous predecessors who did the same, from Judas Iscariot to Ralph Nickleby. Hyde is in part the personification of villainy. Even so, on the tangential question of who is responsible for Hyde's other crimes, even early readers pointed the finger at Jekyll. An 1888 issue of the *Leamington Spa Courier*, for example, reports the sermon of the Rev. Dr. Nicholson, who was one of many clergymen to speak about *Strange Case* from the pulpit. Nicholson distinguishes between "the cultured philosopher" and "the animal," and he rules that the "guilty man was the philosopher."[46] In Freudian terms, Stevenson punishes the ego, not the id. The responsible party is the repressed man who indulges outbursts of excessive vice, not vice itself. Why then do we attribute the final act of destruction to Hyde? Perhaps we are hesitant to do otherwise because we identify more with Jekyll. The nagging implication of his suicide is that what needs repression and purgation is not the animal but the philosopher. Hyde may appear as a figure of degeneration, but it is Jekyll, with his pursuit of esoteric knowledge, his implied love of death, and his fear of life, who better resembles the cliché of degenerated, *fin-de-siècle* decadence.

[46] Quoted in Stevenson, *Strange Case of Dr. Jekyll and Mr. Hyde*, 103.

Before he finishes, Jekyll softens, and he writes of Hyde, "I find it in my heart to pity him" (61). When he catches himself using the pronoun *he*, he admits, "I cannot say, I" (59). The tension here illustrates his failure to hold himself accountable for his actions beyond the self-inflicted punishment of suicide. He is determined to establish a separation between his actions and those of his creation. His use of the third person, his appeal to the pity in his heart—he sounds a little like a reader. There is an analogous relationship here: Hyde is to Jekyll as *Strange Case* is to us. Of all the fictional English suicides documented in this and the previous chapter, his would be the easiest for a middle-class reader to sympathize with. Jekyll falls victim to the temptations that plague anyone who participates in society. His descent into dishonor would strike many as closer to their own experiences. Because he is us, we are able to find it in our hearts to pity him.

In the eighteenth and nineteenth centuries, suicide notes provided readers with insight into self-destruction during a cultural shift in its meaning. For the most part, the fictional suicides of Henry Jekyll and Lady Sibyl Elton resemble those of their mid-Victorian forebearers: these are villains administering their own punishments. Their deaths, however, are neither public nor private but rather somewhere in between. The details are available only to a privileged few, including, of course, the reader. Furthermore, the number of pages turned over to the voices of these suicidal characters distinguishes them from their predecessors in Dickens, Charlotte Brontë, George Eliot, and Thomas Hardy. One would have to look abroad for antecedents in Gustave Flaubert's *Madame Bovary* (1856; translated into English 1881) and later in Leo Tolstoy's *Anna Karenina* (1878; translated into English 1887). The suicide notes in Corelli and Stevenson are still teleological, operating as warnings ("there is No death!") or prompts for reflection ("I cannot say, I"). The causes remain uncontested, the emphasis on the effects. Nevertheless, because they serve these higher moral purposes, the reader is allowed to look closer, and in order to fulfill those purposes, we must look closer at the causes.[47]

[47] Around the turn of the century, several other novelists turned toward fuller representations of the causes of suicide. Grant Allen's *The Woman Who Did* (1895), for example, was published the same year as *The Sorrows of Satan*. The novel is a sympathetic account of a New Woman that ends with her altruistic suicide, a sacrifice from a mother for her daughter. Florence Marryat's *The Blood of the Vampire* (1897) culminates in the same, as the title character, a "psychic vampire" who drains the life from those around her, is a threat to all those she loves (and even those she does not).

3

Make It Vague: The Epistemology of Suicide in *The Man of Property* and *The Good Soldier*

Critics have long remarked that death changed in the twentieth century. Alan Warren Friedman, for example, argues that the prevalence of religious certainty in the nineteenth century made death "definitive, public, and appropriate."[1] He cites as evidence the passing of the *bon vivant* King George IV in 1830, quoting a synopsis from the *Times*: "His Majesty, far from being dismayed by the awful intelligence, received it with the placid resignation of a Christian, and the fortitude of a man" (31). There is a novelistic finality to the scene; one could imagine Dorothea Brooke dying in such a manner. For Friedman, the cumulative blows dealt by the "six horsemen of skepticism"—Marx, Darwin, Nietzsche, Einstein, Arnold van Gennep, and Freud—destroyed the remnants of religious certainty, and their vision of the world was confirmed by the devastation of the First World War. In consequence, modernist authors made death "attenuated, denied, or horrific: initiatory or evaded rather than climatic" (18), while the culture at large ministered to "a conspiracy of silence and willed ignorance" around the matter (61). The Victorian deathbed—"emotionally extravagant, crowded and full of activity" (74)—was now the sterile, indifferent hospital sickroom. Friedman thus gives literary expression to Philippe Ariès's famous argument that fear and an "abdication of the community" had made modern death "invisible."[2] With few exceptions, writes Ariès, "society has banished death."[3]

The professionalization of death in the nineteenth century created the necessary conditions for a conspiracy of silence in the twentieth. In England,

[1] Alan Warren Friedman, *Fictional Death and the Modernist Enterprise* (Cambridge University Press, 1995), i. All subsequent references are noted parenthetically in the text.

[2] Philippe Ariès, *The Hour of Our Death*, trans. Helen Weaver (Barnes & Noble Books, 2000), 612, 559.

[3] Ariès, *The Hour of Our Death*, 560.

the introduction of public mortuaries in the 1850s removed the bodies of the dead from the homes of their families. Coroners were salaried after 1860 and appointed, rather than elected, after 1888. The coroner's officer became a full-time investigator, limiting the need for witnesses at inquests.[4] Juries were persuaded by the increased use of postmortems, pathological analyses, and expert witnesses, and their opinions became less relevant to the verdicts they returned.[5] Beginning in 1907, inquests were no longer held in public houses; they were moved to rooms in public institutions, and then, in busy districts, to coroner's court-houses, adjacent to the mortuary and postmortem room. In 1926, coroners were empowered to hold inquests without juries. Olive Anderson, describing the change, writes that suicide investigations became "shrouded in an atmosphere of officialdom, expertise, and formality [...] a death as suicide had become essentially a matter for a team of experts and professionals."[6] Newspapers reported fewer suicides due to both an increase in other subject matter and changes in the layout of the halfpennies, which became more spacious and did not require "fillers."[7] By the 1890s, the word *suicide* "began to be widely used as a metaphor," as in, *race suicide*.[8] Metaphor requires abstraction, a kind of distance, which is easier when the bodies of the dead no longer remain at home, when knowledge about suicide is conceded to experts, and when the public no longer hosts or participates in the investigation of accidental deaths.

A "conspiracy of silence and willed ignorance" also changed the questions around suicide. The softening of religious dogma reduced interest in debate over damnation. The relaxation of laws and the abolition of punishments resolved most of the arguments about the body and the estate. The professionalization of medicine neutered public opinion, and changes in journalistic and typographical trends reduced the publication of suicide stories in the newspapers. In the following chapter, I will argue that one major modernist response to these changes was to view suicide as a problem of epistemology, as a failure of knowing. Every suicide is produced by a constellation of causes that are impossible to reproduce after the fact. The primary witness is no longer present, and even so, their testimony (including suicide notes) could be disingenuous or misguided. The same applies to the living witnesses. The teleological closure of

4 Olive Anderson, *Suicide in Victorian and Edwardian England* (Clarendon Press, 1987), 257.
5 Anderson, *Suicide in Victorian and Edwardian England*, 257–8.
6 Anderson, *Suicide in Victorian and Edwardian England*, 258–9.
7 Anderson, *Suicide in Victorian and Edwardian England*, 251–2.
8 Anderson, *Suicide in Victorian and Edwardian England*, 336.

the nineteenth century is no longer tenable. There is no Rosetta Stone for suicide. Did the subject choose death? If so, why? Once causes, rather than effects, are contested, they become fertile narrative ground. Novelists like John Galsworthy and Ford Madox Ford appreciated and exploited this epistemological failure. In distinction to their nineteenth-century predecessors, these suicides do not belong to everyone. Rather, the question becomes whether they belong to anyone. "Every time someone dies by his or her own hand," writes Jean Améry, "a veil falls that no one can lift again."[9]

The Man of Property

The climactic suicide in *The Man of Property*, the death of Philip Baynes Bosinney, mostly conforms to the conventions of Victorian fiction. Bosinney is an idealistic architect who has an affair with Irene, wife of the title character, Soames Forsyte. To complicate matters, he is engaged to June Forsyte, another member of the family. Like his predecessors Ralph Nickleby and Lydia Gwilt, Bosinney commits a moral transgression that demands punishment. Like Bertha Mason and John Reed, he is marked for death. His uncle says he has "a streak of his father's Byronism," an easy synonym for the kind of *Sturm und Drang* protagonist who would, like Manfred, court "oblivion, self-oblivion."[10] At a family dinner, Soames looks across the room and sees Bosinney "grinning behind the fumes of his cigarette [… and] shrouded in smoke" (58). Bosinney says of Soames, "*He'll* never blow his brains out," and the stress on *He'll* is left dangling and unanswered (195; emphasis in original). So the means of punishment are suggested. The instrument is suggested, too, in a dress rehearsal for the suicide. When June becomes suspicious of her husband, she visits Bosinney's apartment and spots him across the street: "Their eyes met, and he raised his hat. An omnibus passed, obscuring her view; then, from the edge of the pavement, through a gap in the traffic, she saw him walking on" (211). The tip of the hat is an ambiguous goodbye, since at this point in the novel Bosinney is leaving June for Irene, though not yet for death. Still, the exchange is written as a series

[9] Jean Améry, *On Suicide: A Discourse on Voluntary Death*, trans. John D. Barlow (Indiana University Press, 1999), 8.

[10] John Galsworthy, *The Forsyte Sage*, ed. Geoffrey Harvey (Oxford University Press, 2008), 91. All subsequent references are noted parenthetically in the text. Lord Byron, *The Major Works*, ed. Jerome J. McGann (Oxford University Press, 2008), 279.

of fractured, almost-cinematic images (their eyes meet; the omnibus passes; he is walking on) that, when repeated, will end in his death. "The possibility of self-destruction," writes James Gindin, "is deeply embedded within the texture of the novel."[11] The universe of *The Man of Property* seems to call for Bosinney's destruction—his cigarette smoke goes so far as to form a burial sheet around his face. Under the teleological framework of *Nicholas Nickleby* (1838–9) or *Jane Eyre* (1847), his suicide would serve as a punishment for his sins.

For two reasons, the death is not so simple. First, the values that inform the reception of the suicide have shifted. Young Jolyon, an outsider in his family and something of a Forsyte anthropologist, predicts they will "reject with vigour the suspicion of suicide," instead choosing to view it as "an accident, a stroke of fate," even "an intervention of Providence, a retribution—had not Bosinney endangered their two most priceless possessions, the pocket and the hearth?" (292). The conflation of divinity and finance is characteristic of the Forsytes, who send their wives to church and demonstrate their own piety by paying for pews, "thus expressing in the most practical form their sympathy with the teachings of Christ" (28). Their true religion is earning 4 percent on the principal. When Soames becomes suspicious of his wife, he hires Bosinney to build their country home and then sues him for exceeding the agreed price limit. This is how Soames expresses ownership over Bosinney. Irene he rapes: "the greatest—the supreme act of property," thinks his cousin, George Forsyte (256). The lawsuit for damages and the affair are therefore analogous crimes, crimes of property. Spending your money and sleeping with your wife are differences of degree, not kind. The suicide is still a punishment for adultery, but it is a punishment administered by the owner, not the public or even the divine. This is not atonement for sin but the payment of a trespass fine. It is "the final renunciation of property" (288). In the world of the Forsytes, moral consequences have become financial consequences. The resolution appeals not to the values of middle-class readers but to the interests of landlords.

Consider the first suicide of the novel, which is treated to the severe dogma of commerce. The board of the New Colliery Company, one of old Jolyon's concerns, calls a meeting to discuss "Pippin, their Superintendent, [who] had committed suicide in endeavouring, after his extraordinary two years' silence, to write a letter to his Board" (145). The shareholders are perturbed:

11 James Gindin, *John Galsworthy's Life and Art: An Alien's Fortress* (Macmillan, 1987), 161.

> [The Superintendent] who so—er—ill-advisedly (I say—ill-advisedly) committed suicide, at a time when [...] the agreement which he has so unfortunately cut short with his own hand was for a period of five years, of which one only had expired—I— [...]
>
> I believe I am in order, Mr. Chairman—I ask whether this amount paid, or proposed to be paid, by the Board to the er—deceased—is for services which might have been rendered to the Company—had he not committed suicide? [...]
>
> [O]ur worthy chairman [...] will in some way [...] record our grave disapproval that so promising and valuable a life should have been thus impiously removed from a sphere where both its own interests and—if I may say so—our interests so imperatively demanded its continuance. We should not—nay, we may not—countenance so grave a dereliction of all duty, both human and divine.
>
> (147–8)

Twice the shareholders use the language of Christianity—"impiously removed" and "dereliction of duty, both human and divine"—but the impiety is financial rather than religious. In each case, these condemnations are preceded or followed by the word *interests*. Hence the word *expired* refers not to Pippin but to the term of his "agreement." It is this agreement he has "cut short with his own hand," not his life. The shareholders do not object to Pippin's death; they object to its unprofitable consequences. It is not immoral, it is *ill-advised*. Where suicide was once an affront to God or a theft from the community, it is now a breach of contract. Our bodies belong to the Company, and "dereliction of duty" is the corporate iteration of Plato's argument that a suicide has "quit his station willfully."[12] Under these conditions, it can no longer carry the same kind of meaning. Capital is the dominant ideology, and capital does not read voluntary death as a punishment for sin but as an interruption of work.

Second, the suicide has now been burdened with doubt. Pippin's letter will "be read to the shareholders, who would of course be put into possession of all the facts," but we are not (145). None of the shareholders will speak about its contents, and the superintendent's name appears only one other time in the novel, before the board calls the meeting (45). For our purposes, the two years' silence is permanent. The narrator leaves us to imagine (or not) what he was protesting, though a comment about "the explosion at the mines" provides one

[12] Quoted in Margaret Pabst Battin, ed., *The Ethics of Suicide: Historical Sources* (Oxford University Press, 2015), 311.

avenue of speculation (150). Pippin may have endeavored to write a letter, but he was unsuccessful, since he fails to disseminate it beyond the boardroom. The story of his suicide will at best be filed as an addendum to the confidential minutes of a private corporation. It remains a secret even to the reader. The lack of consideration is more troublesome because it does not include an explanation that sets our doubts to rest. Unlike Charles Dickens, Charlotte Brontë, and George Eliot, who used suicide to resolve a narrative problem, Galsworthy uses it to raise one. Clear lines of cause and effect ("*Done because we are too meny*") have been replaced with em-dashes and ellipses. The ellipsis, denoting omission or unfinished speech, is the punctuation mark best suited to articulate the gaps in knowledge that follow a suicide, and it would later be used to this effect by James Joyce in *Ulysses* (1922) and Aldous Huxley in *Brave New World* (1932).[13]

With Bosinney, the doubt extends beyond the causes of his death to its nature. Despite the discovery of pawn tickets and an overdrawn bank account, the question remains: does he intentionally step in front of the omnibus? Or was this the unfortunate coincidence of poor weather and a distracted mind? The gaps in our knowledge are dramatized through an over-the-shoulder view of George Forsyte, a semi-witness whose vision is obscured by fog and whose hearing is overwhelmed by the sounds of the city. George spots Bosinney "acting under the stress of violent emotion" and thinks, "If the fellow meant to put his 'twopenny' under a bus, he would stop it if he could!" (255). Note the metaphor of money—and not very much money, at that. Soon, however, George shifts from participant to audience. He longs to pluck the sleeves of passersby and tell them, "You don't often see a show like this!" (255). He would even catch them up on the plot, which is itself about the recitation of plot: "Here's a poor devil whose mistress has just been telling him a pretty little story of her husband[...]" (256). When George finally touches Bosinney on the elbow, and Bosinney spins around and asks, "Who are you? What do you want?" he is silent, as if one of

[13] In the penultimate chapter of *Ulysses*, the narrator asks about Rudolph Bloom's suicide note, "What fractions of phrases did the lecture of those five whole words [*To My Dear Son Leopold*] evoke?" The answer reads, "Tomorrow will be a week that I received ... it is no use Leopold to be ... with your dear mother ... that is not more to stand ... to her ... all for me is out ... be kind to Athos, Leopold ... my dear son ... always ... of me ... *das Hertz* ... *Gott* ... *dein*." James Joyce, *Ulysses*, ed. Hans Walter Gabler, Wolfhard Steppe, and Claus Melchior (Vintage, 1986), 595. The last sentence in *Brave New World* describes the hanging of John "the Savage," and the last punctuation mark is an ellipsis: "Slowly, very slowly, like two unhurried compass needles, the feet turned towards the right; north, north-east, east, south-east, south, south-south-south west; then paused, and, after a few seconds, turned as unhurriedly back towards the left. South-south-west, south, south-east, east ... " Aldous Huxley, *Brave New World* (Perennial Library, 1969), 177.

the actors onstage had returned his gaze and demanded an explanation for his prurience (257). The drama thereafter stalls, and boredom pares away his interest. Unlike the suicide notes of the previous chapter, this over-the-shoulder access is no longer revelatory but restrictive. George is startled by a voice, and then a cab, and the narrator relocates to his retelling the story during a game of billiards: "And then [...] I lost him [...] He may be wandering out there now in that fog. If he's not a corpse" (258, 259). On this adulterated evidence, the reader must decide what happened. The novel's free indirect discourse is limited to the Forsytes, who often view Bosinney from a distance. Because we do not have access to his internal monologue, and because we do not even witness his death, we must concede to irresolution. Young Jolyon will argue that "no one so madly in love committed suicide for want of money," but since he does not know about the rape, his answer is drawn from incomplete evidence (292). So is ours. We have purchased an incomplete jigsaw puzzle and we do not even know how many pieces are missing. The point is not which explanation is right; it is that we could not recognize the right explanation even if we saw it. It no longer belongs to us.

The Forsytes, worried about the newspapers, do their part to confuse matters. Young Jolyon predicts the family will "talk of 'that unfortunate accident of young Bosinney's', but perhaps they would not talk—silence might be better!" (292). Both techniques serve them well. Old Jolyon, echoing the halting speech of the shareholders, announces, "There's—some—talk—of—suicide," and his brother James asks, "What should he do that for?" (287). That *for* is typical of the family, a question about the product rather than the motive of his actions. Quite literally, James is asking, what does it profit a man to take his own life? Since "the rumour of suicide" is "against his interest," he insists, "It was an accident! It must have been!" (288). For old Jolyon, the "suspicion of suicide [...] must on no account be entertained" (289), and Soames echoes James, offering the terse explanation, "An accident" (293). A matter of choice thereby becomes a matter of chance. The revision of *suicide* to *accident* eliminates the need for explanation, since accidents are a product of chaos. This is a long-term investment in control over information, one that allows the Forsytes to stifle the words *suicide* and *rape*, neither of which they want associated with their family. It is an act of privatization. The soft power of mutual interest ensures this is the version of events that will be inscribed on Forsyte memory. At the turn of the century, Soames will recall "when that wretched Bosinney was run over," language that implies an accidental reading of his death (357). Around the same time, George's wife will say Irene "had a love affair which ended with the young man's death," open enough to suggest anything from violent death to pneumonia, a Michael Furey to her Gretta Conroy (508). After the First World War, Soames's sister refers to him as "a young man who had got run over" (737), and again he is the object, not the subject, of the sentence. Old Jolyon likewise remembers "poor young Bosinney" (302, 305) as "that young fellow who had got himself run over" (325). The phrasing assigns more agency to the omnibus than its victim, though "had got himself" can still be read as an act of self-destruction. Old Jolyon dies soon after.

Following Bosinney's death, Soames, young Jolyon, and old Jolyon visit the mortuary, a room lit by a single "streak of sunshine smeared along the dustless floor" (289). They see "a form covered by a sheet," which the inspector removes to reveal "a sightless face [...] the sightless defiant face," which prompts each to reflect on "his nature, the odd essential spring, which moved him in fashions minutely, unalterably different from those of every other human being." They stand "far from the others, yet inscrutably close [...] alone with death, silent [...] eyes lowered" (290). Two generations of Forsytes bow their eyes in respect to death, a respect they otherwise reserve only for money. Just as a worm eats of a king, so the Forsytes will one day be humbled by fate, their "odd essential spring" reduced to a sightless face and a form beneath a sheet. Even the light, which illuminates the ground rather than the corpse, accommodates the conceit of partial views. Old Jolyon stands "still as death, his eyes fixed on the body," and the narrator asks, "Who shall tell of what he was thinking?" before listing a series of possible answers. If the narrator cannot be sure, how could we? And if we cannot be sure about this living man, how can we be sure about the dead? Suicide is a provocative illustration, a limit case, of the gulf that exists between all people, locked inside themselves. The inspector, the figure of authority who has made public inquiry obsolete, who is supposed to provide a persuasive, medical answer, refuses to give one: "I don't believe in suicide, nor in pure accident, myself" (291). He produces a lady's handkerchief with the name cut away.

When Galsworthy sent *The Man of Property* to his principal literary advisor, Edward Garnett, Garnett was apoplectic. He wrote that Bosinney's suicide was "psychologically false" and provided a list of reasons to substantiate his claim. These include "it comes near to the average Philistine's conception of 'one of those artist chaps.'"[14] Galsworthy stood by his decision, writing, "Bosinney

[14] Quoted in Gindin, *John Galsworthy's Life and Art*, 157.

commits suicide because of the despairing shock."[15] Nevertheless, the criticism lingered, and after "sleeping or rather not sleeping" on it, he wrote to Garnett that he would leave the question of suicide "vague."[16] Since Galsworthy burned the original manuscripts in 1913, the significance of these changes cannot be determined.[17] Still, in revising Bosinney's death, in taking a conventional Victorian suicide and making it vague, he serves as a fulcrum for a larger transition in English literature and its depiction of voluntary death. Galsworthy denies the reader the ability to say with confidence, "Bosinney commits suicide because of the despairing shock." Witnesses and readers are no longer entitled to such absolute knowledge.

The Good Soldier

The Good Soldier is premised on this conclusion. The narrator, John Dowell, is a semi-witness to two suicides, those of his wife, Florence (née Hurlbird), and his best friend, Edward Ashburnham. Dowell introduces himself to the reader with a series of near-refrains: "I don't know […] I know nothing […] It is all a darkness […] I only know that I am alone—horribly alone."[18] The revelation in Galsworthy's mortuary is here foundational truth. To make matters worse, this is a suicide story told by a man who "know[s] nothing—nothing in the world—of the hearts of men" (12). As for women, he can only guess "what all mothers teach all daughters […] with heart whispering to heart" (13–14). His choice of metaphor is apt: Florence avoids sleeping with Dowell by feigning a heart condition, and this fiction also facilitates her affair with Edward. The hearts of others, both literal and metaphorical, are notoriously illegible to our narrator. Moreover, Dowell is beset by formal challenges. He is unsure how to "put this thing down—whether it would be better to try and tell the story from the beginning, as if it were a story; or whether to tell it from this distance of time, as it reached me from the lips […] of Edward himself" (15). The double meaning of *story* here plays with the slippery distinction between narrativizing and fictionalizing, between recitation and creation, but neither option is particularly

[15] Quoted in Gindin, *John Galsworthy's Life and Art*, 159.
[16] Quoted in Gindin, *John Galsworthy's Life and Art*, 160.
[17] Gindin, *John Galsworthy's Life and Art*, 161.
[18] Ford Madox Ford, *The Good Soldier*, ed. Martin Stannard (Norton, 2012), 12 and 15. All subsequent references are noted parenthetically in the text.

compelling: the worshipful tone of "the lips of [...] Edward himself" implies an ill-placed trust in his friend's honesty. Dowell opts for the latter, a stream-of-consciousness approach that follows his own, belated experience of the events. He never quotes from his diary, and he often relies on second- or third-hand accounts of key moments in the narrative. By constitution and circumstance, Dowell is the worst conceivable candidate to explain a suicide, its causes, and its meaning.

Dowell soon settles on a clear vision of his storytelling—or, more precisely, of his storytelling and his audience:

> I shall just imagine myself for a fortnight or so at one side of the fireplace of a country cottage, with a sympathetic soul opposite me. And I shall go on talking, in a low voice while the sea sounds in the distance and overhead the great black flood of wind polishes the bright stars. From time to time we shall get up and go to the door and look out at the great moon and say: "Why, it is nearly as bright as in Provence!" And then we shall come back to the fireside, with just a touch of a sigh because we are not in that Provence where even the saddest stories are gay. (15)

This is a vision of order in the universe, of harmony between nature and men, collaboration between space and speaker. The sea provides Dowell with a soundtrack, and the wind helps the stars illuminate his scene. We are, no doubt, his candidate for "sympathetic soul," and by the end of this passage we are moving and speaking and sighing in unison. Dowell nonetheless puts limitations on his fantasy: he can imagine himself in a country cottage, but he cannot imagine himself in "that Provence," where the saddest stories are gay. The use of the word *soul* prepares us for the visual echo of Provence and Providence—perhaps his imaginative reach does not extend to interest from the divine. For Dowell, Providence (a word he capitalizes) is a malicious trickster, one who performs "sinister jokes" (44) and is responsible for the "merciless proceedings [...] we call a coincidence" (59). He searches for answers not in the stars but in his manuscript. Kenneth Womack writes that "the novel essentially functions as Dowell's personal act of narrative therapy," and therapy requires an interlocutor.[19] Despite his protestations of being alone, the act of writing betrays some optimism about his project, which is fueled in part by a faith, however qualified, in the value of interpersonal communication. This faith applies not

[19] Kenneth Womack, "'It Is All a Darkness': Death, Narrative Therapy, and Ford Madox Ford's *The Good Soldier*," *Papers on Language & Literature* 38, no. 3 (Summer 2002), 318.

only to his relationship with the reader but also to his relationship with Edward. Dowell believes he can perform an autopsy on his friend, a report on the etiologies of his suicide. If he were convinced without reservation that he knew nothing of the hearts of others, he would not make it beyond the first page. There would be little need to write much else but the refrain. The possibilities and limitations of this encounter—between speaker and listener, narrated by a witness who saw nothing—comprise both the formal and, in terms of suicide, the epistemological spine of *The Good Soldier*. It is all a darkness, and yet I look.

The first mention of suicide in the novel is a denial, establishing what will become a consistent uncertainty around the action. Edward's lover Maisie Maidan overhears him speaking to his new lover, Florence, and Dowell describes her subsequent death in detail:

> Maisie had died in the effort to strap up a great portmanteau. She had died so grotesquely that her little body had fallen forward into the trunk and it had closed upon her; like the jaws of a gigantic alligator [...] Her dark hair, like the hair of a Japanese had come down and covered her body and her face. Leonora lifted her up [...] and laid her on the bed with her hair about her. She was smiling as if she had just scored a goal in a hockey match. You understand, she had not committed suicide. Her heart had just stopped. I saw her, with the long lashes on the cheeks, with the smile about the lips, with the flowers all about her.
>
> (58)

His denial is peculiar. Why does Dowell need to tell us that she had not committed suicide when no one has suggested that she had? We are, as he keeps reminding us, his "silent listener," and any suspicions on the part of the reader would be the product of his imagination (42, 106, 124, and 134). "You understand" introduces further ambiguity: its assumed authority has a nervous, desperate quality, and the sentence is ordered so he tells us *that* we understand before he tells us *what* we understand. Did Maisie Maidan commit suicide? The question is unanswerable, but it puts pressure on Dowell's version of events. The girl who was eaten by the alligator trunk, her modesty preserved by her Japanese hair? His credulity strains credulity. How could he know? In the final sentence quoted above, the setting shifts from the site of Maisie's death to her that of her funeral. Dowell fails to mark the transition. When he first mentions her smile, he is referring to her fresh corpse. When he mentions it the second time, after an ambiguous "I saw her," he has pivoted from deathbed to casket. This implies a continuity between the body on discovery and its presentation for an audience. It also invites the misunderstanding that he witnessed both, a misunderstanding he prepares for a few pages earlier when he writes, "We found her dead when we got back" (53). In fact, Leonora found her. At the funeral, Dowell describes Maisie holding the stem of a white lily in her hand. She looks like "a bride in the sunlight of the mortuary candles," and he compares "the white coifs of the two nuns that knelt at her feet" to "swans that were to bear her away to kissing-kindness land" (58). In his rendering, her symbolic virginity shrouds her literal death, and a fairy-tale narrative sends her off to marriage rather than oblivion. She even seems pleased about it all, if we are to believe that the corpse was smiling. (This would be an unusual choice for an Edwardian funeral—or for a woman dying of a heart attack.) The inverted, figurative language dresses up Maisie's death as new life, and a woman who died "grotesquely" is buried besieged by flowers, her countenance lit by artificial metaphors ("mortuary candles") for a natural phenomenon ("the sunlight"). From this tableau, Dowell draws his authority. Why should we privilege his story over the suggestive possibilities of his denial? At the very least, "kissing-kindness land" should encourage us to read the scene with some irony.

In *The Good Soldier*, then, suicide is indeterminate, unstable. A suicide story is never over. Soon we will read that Nancy's mother "committed suicide owing to the brutalities of her father" before learning, much later, that she is alive and well (70). Even in the ancillary suicides, Ford cannot help but sow confusion. Ultimately, the absence of testimony, of first-hand evidence, condemns all suicide narratives to a fundamentally imaginative gesture, one which must answer the questions: why did it happen, what did it feel like, and what does it mean? On all three, we are working with limited evidence. We are faced with an epistemological challenge. So we have to make something up. Moreover, all private scenes become public once they are recounted, particularly once they are written down. They become stories, and in all public accounts of voluntary death, the motivations of the storyteller eclipse the experiences of the suicide. Even if it were possible to access the thoughts of the deceased, the game of telephone we play with our friends and loved ones, our memories, and our self-delusions would soon distort the original experience. Say Dowell did witness the death, the discovery of the body, even the private moments of Maisie's affair with Edward. Could he be trusted to record it with accuracy?

Dowell's account of Florence's suicide is characterized by a combination of confusion and indifference. His initial impressions of the night of her death are unenlightening, muddled by "circumstances of clamour, of outcry, of the crash of many people running together" (77). The presence of the Grand Duke, the chief of the police, and the hotelkeeper, M. Schontz, all of whom likely know the truth before Dowell, prevent him from learning it himself. The community that used to play an integral role in making sense of suicide is here clutter and even an obstacle to revelation—Dowell has "no possible guide" to the scene. His first draft of the events is assembled through pieces. The juxtaposition of Florence "running with a white face and with one hand over her heart" with her "lying upon her bed with the so familiar little brown flask clenched in her fingers" leads him to believe that she died of heart troubles, a failure in storytelling that demands the audience infer connections between disconnected images. It is the deceit of montage. After he has been informed of the facts, he reconstructs the scene as follows:

> She ran upstairs, arranged herself decoratively upon her bed—she was a sweetly pretty woman with smooth pink and white cheeks, long hair, the eyelashes falling like a tiny curtain on her cheeks. She drank the little phial of prussic acid and there she lay.—O, extremely charming and clear-cut—looking with a puzzled expression at the electric-light bulb that hung from the ceiling, or perhaps through it, to the stars above. Who knows? Anyhow, there was an end of Florence.
>
> (86)

Vincent J. Cheng notes there is a "symmetry and similarity" between the deaths of Florence and Masie Maiden, as both are precipitated by overheard conversations.[20] This time, Florence overhears Edward speaking to Nancy Rufford, the newest, unconsummated object of his affections. Both are apparent heart attacks, and the scenes also overlap in their use of language: the "eyelashes falling [...] on her cheeks" echoes Maisie's "long lashes on the cheeks," and that "O" has the same strained theatricality of his description of Maisie's burial. Dowell's response, however, is neither symmetrical nor similar. When the victim is Florence, he is not taken in by the artifice. He is cynical about this fairy tale. She was, after all, "always playacting," mimicking "the heroine of a French comedy" or "one of the great erotic women of whom history tells us" (85). For Dowell, this is all a play she has written for herself, and now its "tiny curtain" has fallen on the "decorative" denouement. She even provides her own prop, the "little phial of prussic acid" that had been dressed to look like amyl nitrate. Unlike Maisie's "little body," these diminutives are scornful rather than affectionate. What can

[20] Vincent J. Cheng, "A Chronology of *The Good Soldier*," *English Language Notes* 24 (September 1986), 93.

we conclude about Florence's suicide? Very little. Her "puzzled expression" is an irresolute counterpart to Maisie's smile, and the "electric-light bulb," concealing the stars above, is even more artificial than her candles. Her prop is well-chosen—as Venetia Abdalla writes, poison is "deceitful and secretive," prone to masquerade, multivalent, and "elusive, hard to pin down, like Florence."[21]

The clues are tantalizing, but they are never assembled into a satisfying whole. Dowell seems to have little interest in exploring the meaning of her suicide. There is the shrug of "Who knows?" and the curt dismissal, "Anyhow, there was the end of Florence." He does not even consider himself a participant in the action, and he claims preventing her suicide "would have been like chasing a scrap of paper" (97). The metaphor evokes our own relationship to the novel as well as his earlier description of the moments before her death, when he saw her "running with a face whiter than paper" (74). Abdalla writes of this moment, "it is as if she has quite literally taken over the function of the text."[22] If so, he fails to read it, and in consequence so do we. Our understanding is restricted by his indifference. As for the public narrative of her death, Dowell cedes it to others. He is tasked with spending her inheritance, which he would like to donate to "the relief of sufferers from the heart," since she "had certainly died of her heart, as I saw it" (134). So she gets the ending she would want, after all—perhaps. One of her aunts suggests giving the money to lung-patients, and the other tells Dowell to keep it, she does not want the Hurlbird name perpetuated. He misunderstands this comment until Leonora tells him that Florence left a letter on her dressing-table, something he must have missed when he viewed the corpse. Since the letter is addressed to her aunt, he assumes she must have read "a good bit about Edward Ashburnham," and he attributes her reluctance over the Hurlbird name to whatever she must have read (133). What did she read? Dowell appears reasonable but uncurious about the note: "I can quite understand that she would not like to go out of the world without making some comments." The emotional rather than the practical details of the affair, which could in turn illuminate the causes of the suicide, remain out of our reach. There are echoes here of Geoffrey Tempest's discovery of Lady Sibyl Elton's body in *The Sorrows of Satan* (1895), but in this case, the reader is left as ignorant as the narrator. Florence, who was in life an "unstoppable talker," is rendered

[21] Venetia Abdalla, "*The Good Soldier*: A Tale of Poison. Lethal Little Bottles in the Work of Ford Madox Ford and Violent Hunt," in *Ford Madox Ford's The Good Soldier: Centenary Essays*, ed. Max Saunders and Sara Haslam (Brill, 2015), 198, 199.

[22] Abdalla, "*The Good Soldier*: A Tale of Poison," 204.

silent (126). Likewise, her legacy is left unsettled, at least for us. Dowell tells his attorney to sort it out with the aunts and leaves the country. We never learn whether she is remembered for her generosity to heart-patients or lung-patients or no patients at all. The teleological explanation (*she died so others who suffered like she could live*) is invoked but left unresolved.

The suicide does offer Dowell one moment of enlightenment. Compare his reactions to Florence's affair and her suicide, which serve as parallel sentences. After Edward dies, Leonora makes a casual reference to "your wife [...] my husband's mistress," and he writes, "That was how I got the news—full in the face, like that" (76). Then Leonora says, "I think it was stupid of Florence to commit suicide," and Dowell uses a different word: "So that that was the first knowledge I had that Florence had committed suicide" (77). The affair is news, gossip exchanged by those who were not present. He compares it to hearing "Mrs. So-and-So is *au mieux* with a certain gentleman" (76). The suicide, on the other hand, demands language that evokes the fall of man, and it establishes a level of truthfulness between Dowell and Leonora that he never shared with his wife. After she speaks, Dowell recognizes their connection and "knew then that Leonora was about to let me into her full confidence" (77). The biblical definition of *knowing* has been reversed. Dowell has never learned anything about or from desire, and it is instead death that creates knowledge. The chaste Dowell learns the circumstances of Florence's suicide while the promiscuous Edward is protected by his ignorance of her character: he assumes she would not kill herself "without writing at least a tirade to him" (92). (Edward, it seems, does not learn much from desire, either.) For Dowell, the suicides of his wife and his best friend have provided an occasion for intimacy, an intimacy that was absent during his years of friendship with Leonora, since her silence (about sex, no less) prevented the affinity that may develop between the spouses of adulterers. Still, this exchange does little to enlighten him about the causes of the suicide. The parallel sentences have a second difference. "That was how I got the news" follows a paragraph break, while "So that was the first knowledge" follows a section break. Both suggest a pause. Dowell may be taking a moment to assimilate the information, to determine how to frame it, but the second sentence follows a literal blank, a line of white where text might be. A typographical iteration of the refrain, it is all a darkness.

On Edward's suicide, Dowell is clear and sentimental. There is even the dress rehearsal. Edward's wife, Leonora, confronts him about his love for Nancy, offers him a divorce, and then is overcome with fear that he "must have committed suicide" (143). She goes to his room and sees him "oiling the breech action of a gun [...] an unusual thing for him to do, at that time of night, in his evening clothes." He looks at her, "his face illuminated by the light cast upwards from the round orifices in the green candle shades" (143). This is stock Victorian imagery, an announcement of the inevitable, complete with a light cast on the condemned and the ominous gun preparing us for news of an "accident." Dowell, meanwhile, is a privileged witness, the last to see Edward alive. They are in the stables together when Edward receives a telegram from Nancy, who has been sent abroad after Leonora informed her about Edward's "career and character" (162). Their relationship was chaste, and he is devastated to have lost her respect. Her telegram is succinct and betrays no grief over the separation: "Safe Brindisi. Having rattling good time. Nancy" (169). Considering she is paying by the word, that *rattling* must hurt. Edward "regarded it without emotion," but then he "looked up to the roof of the stable, as if he were looking to Heaven, and whispered something that I did not catch." He removes a pen-knife from his pocket and suggests Dowell "might just take that wire to Leonora." When he realizes Dowell will not interfere with his suicide, "his eyes became soft and almost affectionate," and he bids his friend farewell: "So long, old man, I must have a bit of a rest, you know." Dowell is tempted to respond, "God bless you," but he says nothing in deference to "English good form."

Cause and effect are presented here with a clarity that is uncharacteristic of our narrator: the telegram is followed by the pen-knife, which is followed by the request that Dowell leave. The kindness of the euphemism ("a bit of a rest") is reminiscent of the metaphors Dowell used for Maisie Maidan. Moreover, the silence, the mutual understanding—this is a deathbed scene that depicts Dowell as Edward's priest. Earlier in the novel, after dismissing the importance of the "sex-instinct," Dowell argues that "the real fierceness of desire, the real heat of passion" is in a man's "craving for identity with the woman that he loves" (82). It is the desire "to see with the same eyes, to touch with the same sense of touch, to hear with the same ears, to lose his identity." He could, of course, be describing his relationship to the reader, as this was the appeal of the suicide note, but he is also describing how he perceives his relationship to Edward, with whom he attempts to identify throughout *The Good Soldier*. He writes, "I love him because he was just myself," right before it "suddenly occurs" to him that he has "forgotten to say how Edward met his death"—another gentle euphemism, since it implies fate rather than choice (168). If there is passion to be found in our narrator, it is in this friendship. His authority on Edward's suicide is his evidence of that passion.

Nevertheless, the perennial question returns: should we trust him? The story is very neat, and it is suspicious that Dowell claims that it "suddenly occurs" to him, in the last few paragraphs of the novel, that he has "forgotten to say how Edward met his death," as if this were not the culmination of his entire project (168). Note, too, that each time he implies that he understands something, he hedges: it is *as if* Edward were praying to heaven, his eyes become *almost* affectionate. And the tableau with the gun is a red herring, of sorts. Unlike Bosinney, Edward chooses a different instrument the second time around. He is also lit from below, not above, reversing the meaning of the traditional redemptive metaphor. The filtered, artificial light, the green face, these hardly evoke the atonement of someone like Thomas Hood's Unfortunate. At the beginning of *The Good Soldier*, Dowell complains that "the modern English habit of taking every one for granted is a good deal to blame" for his ignorance, since "with all the taking for granted, you never really get an inch deeper than the things I have catalogued" (32). His reading of this final interaction with Edward is predicated on precisely those cultural silences—he is taking Edward for granted here—and this enables Dowell to write it however he would like: Edward, after all, is not there to contradict his insistence on mutual affection. The implement, a *pen*-knife, is a mischievous pun. Dowell is auditioning to play Edward's sympathetic soul, his narrator, but sympathy and truthfulness are not necessarily synonyms.

The neatness is further complicated by Dowell's two prior explanations for the suicide. In the first, Leonora "made him a terrible scene" about his latest expenditure, two hundred pounds on another young woman (132). She "had the vague idea" that his experience with Nancy "ought to have taught Edward lesson—the lesson of economy," so she threatens to take his bank account away from him. Dowell writes, "I guess that made him cut his throat. He might have stuck it out otherwise [...] he could be of no public service ... Well, it finished him." The explanation is poetic—there is no greater economy than suicide, as Father Time demonstrates—and it enables Leonora, a Catholic, to remarry and find happiness. This is the teleological explanation. So is his second, where he ventriloquizes nineteenth-century platitudes: "The villains—for obviously Edward and the girl [Nancy] were villains—have been punished by suicide and madness" (166). No surprise from a man whose "sentimentalism required of him an attitude of Byronic gloom" (113). *Byronic gloom*, the well-worn sign of self-destructiveness, has been drained of its significance through repetition—it is a requirement rather than a chosen affectation or a sincere expression of emotion. Dowell continues, "Society must go on, I suppose, and society can only exist if [...] the passionate, the headstrong, and the too-truthful are condemned to suicide and to madness" (167–8). Whether Edward is villainous or passionate, the rules of the game are fixed, as if they were characters in a script: "The end was perfectly plain to each of them [...] Edward must die, the girl must lose her reason because Edward died" (155). The emphasis is on the punishment and its consequences. Ralph Nickleby was such a villain, Nicholas the embodiment of the society that must go on, his marriage a ritual to symbolize that going on. Dowell does not seem especially persuaded by these views, but he voices them nonetheless. The purpose here is not to determine the truth, nor to determine which version of the causes of Edward's suicide is closest to the truth. It is to illustrate the futility of such questions, especially when they are answered by a compromised speaker.

Consider the line quoted above, in fuller context: "I love him because he was just myself. If I had had the courage and the virility and possibly also the physique of Edward Ashburnham I should, I fancy, have done much what he did" (168). No doubt had his mother been Queen Victoria and his father Prince Albert, he would have been just like King Edward, too. The absurdity of this claim reveals how much Dowell's sense of Edward is tied to a false sense of himself. This declaration of kinship follows the similar delusion that "I myself, in my fainter way, come into the category of the passionate, of the headstrong, and the too-truthful." Our Dowell, the "what is called the sex instinct" Dowell (29)? Even allowing for his idiosyncratic definition of passion, are we really meant to believe that he is headstrong or too-truthful? Moreover, what does he know about Edward's courage and virility? Despite spending a great deal of time together for a decade, his evidence of genuine contact, of a sincere friendship with the man is virtually nonexistent. Take, for example, the importance of letters to this novel: Edward's marriage is negotiated through letters (96–7); his affair with Mrs. Basil is discovered when her husband "got hold of [...] some letters and things" (118); he continues, after their separation, to "write her long letters" (123); Leonora asserts a right to open Edward's mail after she mistakenly opens a letter from his blackmailer (44–5); and, of course, it is a telegram from Nancy that precipitates Edward's suicide. Letters form a network of knowledge exchange from which Dowell is excluded. His letters are to the *Times*, not to people. He never reads Florence's letter, perhaps a suicide note, and he never once mentions, let alone quotes, a letter from his friend. Yet Edward himself clearly relies on letters as a form of intimacy: he is convinced that both Maisie and Florence died of heart failure because of the absence any, and he continues to write to Mrs. Basil even after their affair has ended (123).

As a matter of fact, Edward's voice is mostly absent from *The Good Soldier*, despite Dowell's insistence on their relationship as secret sharers. He may talk "like a cheap novelist," but we never hear it (79). Dowell insists that Edward "never told a story that couldn't have gone into the columns of the *Field* more than once or twice in all the nine years of my knowing him" (14). He tells neither the stories that could nor the stories that could not. Later, when Edward hears that Nancy is leaving for India, Dowell writes, "And that evening Edward spoke to me," but the line is followed by a section break and a digression about Edward and Leonora (136). Later, the night before Edward has to drive Nancy to the station, he tells Dowell, "I am so desperately in love with Nancy Rufford that I am dying of it," one of only two sentences from this conversation that Dowell will quote—the other is "Look here, old man, I wish you would drive with Nancy and me to the station to-morrow" (165). The section ends, "He talked all night." Like a gentleman demurring over a description of a sexual encounter, Dowell skips their evening conversation and picks up his story in the morning. We hear none of Edward's talk. We instead hear a great deal of Dowell's. The final scene of the novel tells us a little about our narrator and even less about his protagonist. If the suicide remains a site of revelation, it is a revelation about the character of the witness, not the victim.

Recall the first time Dowell spots Edward, when he gushes, "His face hitherto had, in the wonderful English fashion, expressed nothing whatever. Nothing. There was in it neither joy nor despair; neither hope nor fear; neither boredom nor satisfaction [...] I never came across such a perfect expression before and I never shall again" (24). For Dowell, this nothingness represents an opportunity. Like a Rorschach inkblot, Edward can be anyone he wants him to be, and he will eventually fill that face with joy, despair, hope, fear, and boredom—though perhaps not satisfaction. Its perfection resides in its blankness. Dowell later declares, "We are all so afraid, we are all so alone, we all so need from the outside the assurance of our own worthiness to exist" (83). In Edward, he has found this outside assurance, with the added advantage that he gets to write both parts. Such is true of any suicide, and Edward's is not the only one in which Dowell claims a special if unrealized role. When recounting Florence's death, he insists he could have saved her life: "It is even possible that, if that feeling had not possessed me, I should have run up sooner to her room and might have prevented her drinking the prussic acid" (86–7). Here is the same rhetorical trick he used to compare himself to Edward—*if* he had not been struck by the feeling that she "was a personality of paper [...] she wasn't real; she was just a mass of talk out of guidebooks, of drawings out of fashion-plates," he would have prevented her death (86). Dowell asserts control over her suicide even as he does not exercise that control. At the end of *The Good Soldier*, he again asserts control, this time over Edward and Edward's death. He is the monkish translator of the silent suicide note. Florence is not the only personality of paper; language by necessity turns all of us into such. Like Narcissus, when Dowell looks, he only sees himself. Of the suicide around which he circles again and again and again, we know nothing.

The professionalization of death in the twentieth century and the "conspiracy of silence and willed ignorance" that followed made suicide an attractive subject for modernist novelists, whose works have long been categorized by formal innovations that lend themselves to illustrating the failure of knowing it provokes: multiple and subjective narrators, nonlinear structures, irresolute conclusions. Like other twentieth-century deaths, suicide was banished from society, and in consequence the public no longer held a significant role in fashioning its meaning. Privacy breeds irreconcilable stories and epistemological doubt. The deaths of Edward Ashburnham, Florence Dowell, Philip Baynes Bosinney, and even Maisie Maidan are either inaccessible to the reader or altogether impossible to comprehend. Left unresolved, it is their causes, far more than their effects—either criminal or divine—that are in dispute. The chorus chanting in unison ("We heard him call 'Bertha!' We saw him approach her") is succeeded by the widower, alone, confessing aloud to no one.

4

Entering Other Lives: Virginia Woolf and the Suicidal Character

Before she wrote *Mrs. Dalloway* (1925), Virginia Woolf was bothered by a problem of consciousness: the inability to occupy the minds of others. On vacation in Bayreuth, she wrote to her sister, "I am haunted by the thought that I can never know what anyone is feeling," attributing it to her age—she is 27.[1] At thirty, four weeks before she accepted Leonard's proposal, she wrote to him, "You seem so foreign [...] I sometimes feel that no one ever has or ever can share something."[2] She makes the observation about Katherine Mansfield ("Strange how little we know our friends"),[3] an old admirer ("But how even begin to guess another's feelings?"),[4] and two women she watches dining in silence with their mother ("I could not say what went forward in those mute minds").[5] When the subject comes up in a letter to the writer Gerald Brenan, she switches from the second to the third person, presumably to emphasize their distance, asking him, "What is he thinking? How does it feel to be inside him? I am tormented by my own ignorance of his mind."[6] Thus, between about 1909 and 1923, Woolf believed that "the existence of life in another human being is as difficult to realise as a play of Shakespeare when the book is shut."[7] This had inevitable consequences

1 Virginia Woolf, *The Letters of Virginia Woolf Volume One: 1882–1912*, ed. Nigel Nicolson and Joanne Trautmann (Harvest, 1975), 404.

2 Virginia Woolf, *The Diary of Virginia Woolf Volume One: 1915–1919*, ed. Anne Olivier Bell (Harvest/HBJ, 1977), 496.

3 Virginia Woolf, *The Diary of Virginia Woolf Volume Two: 1920–1924*, ed. Anne Olivier Bell (Harvest, 1978), 62.

4 Woolf, *Diary Two*, 130.

5 Woolf, *Diary Two*, 47.

6 Virginia Woolf, *The Letters of Virginia Woolf Volume Three: 1923–1928*, ed. Nigel Nicolson and Joanne Trautmann (Harcourt Brace Jovanovich, 1978), 66.

7 Woolf, *Diary One*, 186.

for her fiction, which was moving from a more conventional realism toward a stream-of-consciousness prose that "should make us feel ourselves seated at the centre of another mind."[8] The image here, with the reader as audience to the consciousness of a character, a kind of Cartesian theater, suggests that fiction can provide the intimacy Woolf despairs of in her diary and her letters.

During the composition of *Mrs. Dalloway*, Woolf addressed her concerns in two essays, "Mr. Bennett and Mrs. Brown" (1923) and "Character in Fiction" (1924), where she analyzes the failure of Edwardian novelists to write characters that are "real, true, and convincing."[9] Confronted with a change in human character on or about December 1910, Arnold Bennett and his contemporaries retreated, offering their readers "a vast sense of things in general" in exchange for "a very vague one of things in particular," sacrificing intimacy for scope (387). Bennett, for example, constructs his vast sense through the accumulation of materialist details. Reading the first few pages of *Hilda Lessways* (1911), Woolf writes, "We cannot hear her mother's voice, or Hilda's voice; we can only hear Mr. Bennett's voice telling us facts about rents and freeholds and copyholds and fines" (430). His characters are buried under the minutiae of their social and historical contexts. To further illustrate, Woolf invokes the figure of Mrs. Brown, a middle-class woman on the train from Richmond to Waterloo. Woolf overhears some of her conversation but none, of course, of her thoughts. To compensate, Bennett would obsess over the advertisements, the cushions, the brooch she wears, its cost, and the location of purchase. He would assemble his character through the objects that surround her. This enables Bennett to "gradually sidle" toward Mrs. Brown, but he will never seat his readers at the center of her mind (429). Woolf admits that she has diagnosed the illness without offering a cure: "I let my Mrs. Brown slip through my fingers. I have told you nothing whatever about her" (432). The task before her contemporaries is to "create solid, living, flesh-and-blood Mrs. Brown," to restore character in fiction (388).

Woolf soon made her first venture into sustained stream-of-consciousness prose with Clarissa Dalloway, another middle-class woman identified by her married name. With Septimus Warren Smith, the lovesick, shell-shocked war veteran, she tested the limits of this experiment: the representation of madness and suicide. For the novel to succeed, the reader must believe we are sharing

[8] Virginia Woolf, Review of Dorothy Richardson's *The Tunnel*, *The Essays of Virginia Woolf: Volume Three:1919–1924*, ed. Andrew McNeillie (Harcourt, 1988), 11.

[9] Woolf, *Essays Three*, 421. All subsequent references to "Mr. Bennett and Mrs. Brown" and "Character in Fiction" are noted parenthetically in the text.

a view of "the world seen by the sane & the insane side by side."[10] We must feel seated at the center of their minds. If successful, stream-of-consciousness resolves all the problems that "haunted" and "tormented" Woolf in her personal life: it makes the foreign familiar, it makes "mute minds" speak. Septimus's thoughts, his motivations, and the precipitating actions, all are clear. Woolf does not obscure his suicide in a fog of epistemological doubt. At issue is what follows: in the novel's penultimate scene, Clarissa envisions Septimus's death and experiences an epiphany; as a result, she feels "somehow very like him."[11] Because of what Molly Hite calls Woolf's "tonal ambiguities," the reader is left unsure of how to react.[12] Should we consider this epiphany, this moment of communion, genuine? The answer has great bearing on whether Woolf's formal choices meet the demands of her subject matter. As a pseudo-witness to his suicide, and as the recipient of a series of associated images and impressions, Clarissa stands in for the reader—her vicarious experience of his death is not unlike our own. If her epiphany is genuine, if she and Septimus do "share something," then fiction can offer the illusion of unmediated intimacy that real life denies us. We can even know the mind of a suicide.

Woolf's Other Fictional Suicides

The relationship between Clarissa and Septimus—and the relationship between Septimus and the reader—is unique in the Woolf canon. Septimus was her first published fictional suicide, and for the remainder of her career, the suicides of her characters were cameos and ghosts. Consider *Orlando* (1928), where voluntary death is used as a polemical tool, and the death of the suicidal character is less important than its political valence. Woolf writes, "The life of the average [nineteenth-century] woman was a succession of childbirths," and then illustrates through the story of a memoirist: "Eusebius Chubb shall be our witness to the effect this all had upon the mind of a sensitive man who could do nothing to stop it."[13] One morning, Chubb writes thirty-five folio pages "all about

[10] Woolf, *Diary Two*, 207.

[11] Virginia Woolf, *Mrs. Dalloway*, ed. Anne E. Fernald (Cambridge University Press, 2014), 166. All subsequent references are noted parenthetically in the text.

[12] Molly Hite, *Woolf's Ambiguities: Tonal Modernism, Narrative Strategy, Feminist Precursors* (Cornell University Press, 2017).

[13] Virginia Woolf, *Orlando*, ed. Suzanne Raitt and Ian Blyth (Cambridge University Press, 2018), 209.

nothing," then goes to his garden, where he is overwhelmed by its fecundity, which reminds him of his own: his wife is giving birth to their fifteenth child. Chubb's death receives a single, unfussy sentence: "He went indoors, wrote the passage quoted above, laid his head in a gas oven, and when they found him later he was past revival."[14] The story is in part a joke, as it emphasizes the pain of the man who fathered the children over the woman who birthed and raised them. Chubb's failure to produce as a writer also works to undermine the pathos of his death, and the claim that he could "do nothing to stop it" is, at least in the strictest sense, false. Nevertheless, there is sincerity mixed in with the irony. His suicide remains an indictment of the culture that has transformed his wife into a machine that produces babies. Still, despite the promise about "the mind of a sensitive man," and despite the record Chubb leaves behind, our insight is limited (an irony considering he is a memoirist).

The suicide of Judith Shakespeare, the fictional sister of William Shakespeare in *A Room of One's Own* (1929), is wholly sincere, but it is still used primarily as evidence, in this case to demonstrate that "it would have been impossible, completely and entirely, for any woman to have written the plays of Shakespeare in the age of Shakespeare."[15] While her educated brother leaves a wife and child in Stratford to "practic[e] his art on the boards," his "extraordinarily gifted sister" is discouraged from books, coerced into a marriage she flees, and laughed out of the London theaters. In the end, Judith "found herself with child" and "killed herself one winter's night and lies buried at some cross-roads where the omnibuses now stop outside the Elephant and Castle" (48). Woolf concludes:

> When [...] one reads of a witch being ducked, of a woman possessed by devils, of a wise woman selling herbs [...] then I think we are on the track of a lost novelist, a suppressed poet, of some mute and inglorious Jane Austen, some Emily Brontë who dashed her brains out on the moor or mopped and mowed about the highways crazed with the torture that her gift had put her to (48–9).

Crossroads, as mentioned in Chapter 1, were used as burial sites to disorient revenants, to prevent resurrected suicides from returning home. In this context, the practice assumes sinister associations with the Oxbridge men who deny the narrator admission to their libraries. Judith's suicide is a poetic injustice, and the treatment of her corpse, buried out of the churchyard and beneath a center

[14] Woolf, *Orlando*, 210.

[15] Virginia Woolf, *A Room of One's Own* (Harvest, 2005), 46; emphasis added. All subsequent references are noted parenthetically in the text.

of metropolitan commerce, a grim metaphor for all the suppressed voices of her contemporaries. Since her function is symbolic—she is the "any woman" of Woolf's argument—she resists close characterization. Her suicide is meant to prompt outrage and perhaps political action. Like "the mute and inglorious Jane Austen," Judith Shakespeare herself never speaks, and like Eustace Chubb, her story is limited to a single, albeit a longer, paragraph.

The sketch "The Fascination of the Pool" (1929) describes how an observer, were they to look into the water, would hear some of the "fancies, complaints, and confidences" that have been dropped into it over the centuries.[16] One of these "liquid thoughts" bubbles to the surface, and it belongs to a girl from the summer of 1662, who remembers the heat, the soldiers, and her lover. A second bubbles and glances back at the girl, whose death is recorded between the non-essential bookends of parentheses: "(for she had drowned herself)."[17] Critics have read this pool as a metaphor of the face,[18] the mind,[19] the writer's mind,[20] and writing itself,[21] as each have depths from which something occasionally breaches. Most emphasize its ego-blurring effect on both the observer and the reader, almost with a tone of approval. Claudia Olk, for example, writes that the "gaze into the pool creates communion with other minds,"[22] and Melba Cuddy-Keane, that it "draws the reader into a moment of unification and sharing, enacting a liquid merging of different selves as the narrator slips from one pronoun to another [...] reducing the friction of the barriers of consciousness."[23] This is true. The pool does seem to act as the center of a mind, dispatching messages to the surface, and the image is a near-literal representation of stream-of-consciousness. The voices stretch across centuries, and they share intimate details of their lives; the anonymous girl even speaks a few sentences. The sketch appears to fulfill Woolf's desire for two people to "share something," in this case, the observer or the reader and the voices that populate her pool. Even so, there is a problem of vantage. "The Fascination of the Pool" is shallow by design: its first line reads,

16 Virginia Woolf, *The Complete Shorter Fiction of Virginia Woolf*, ed. Susan Dick (Harvest, 1989), 226.
17 Woolf, *Complete Shorter Fiction*, 227.
18 Kamila Pawlikowska, *Anti-Portraits: Poetics of the Face in Modern English, Polish and Russian Literature (1835–1965)* (Brill, 2015), 169.
19 Melba Cuddy-Keane, *Virginia Woolf, the Intellectual, and the Public Sphere* (Cambridge University Press, 2003), 125.
20 Christine Reynier, *Virginia Woolf's Ethics of the Short Story* (Palgrave Macmillan, 2009), 131.
21 Laura Marcus, "The Short Fiction," in *A Companion to Virginia Woolf*, ed. Jessica Berman (Wiley Blackwell, 2016), 30.
22 Claudia Olk, *Virginia Woolf and the Aesthetics of Vision* (De Gruyter, 2014), 101.
23 Cuddy-Keane, *Virginia Woolf, the Intellectual, and the Public Sphere*, 130.

"It may have been very deep—certainly one could not see to the bottom of it."[24] The reader is not seated at the center of this mind but its surface. The liquid thoughts are superficial, too brief and with too little context to contain much meaning. As Lecia Rosenthal writes, "what is held in common is also, despite its communicative flow, never quite shared or transparent."[25] In the case of the girl who drowned herself, we are left without the connective tissue of her narrative, only the implication that her love might have been the cause of her death and the pool its instrument. The soldiers remain an ominous, background mystery. The suicide is evocative rather than substantial; we must supply the missing information.

Woolf would use the same image for the almost same purpose over a decade later, in *Between the Acts* (1941). A scullery maid, "cooling her cheeks" by a lily pond, is reminded of a downstairs superstition: "It was in that deep centre, in that black heart, that the lady had drowned herself. Ten years since the pool had been dredged and a thigh bone recovered. Alas, it was a sheep's, not a lady's [...] the servants insisted, they must have a ghost; the ghost must be a lady's; who had drowned herself for love."[26] The suicide is fodder for gossip, evocative not for the reader but for the characters, who demand their story despite the disappointment of the facts. The deep center is metaphorical, not literal, and dredging does not yield its black heart.

A late story, "The Legacy" (1940), reads like *The Good Soldier* (1915), condensed. Angela Clandon is hit and killed by a car, and her husband, Gilbert, a member of parliament, manages her estate in the aftermath. Angela has remembered everyone, "even Sissy Miller, her secretary," to whom she has left a pearl brooch.[27] To Gilbert, she leaves her diary, "the only thing they had not shared when she was alive" (281). The reader follows Gilbert through a series of revelations, many of which are apparent to us long before they are to him: his wife was unhappy, she wanted a child, she was having an affair, her lover (B. M.) was a socialist, he committed suicide, and she did the same. Like Dowell, Gilbert is an ignorant cuckold, and the suicide of his wife represents the culmination of his ignorance, an illustration of his failure to know her true character—a lesson in "the necessity of attempting to enter into the minds of other people," writes

[24] Woolf, *Complete Shorter Fiction*, 226.

[25] Lecia Rosenthal, *Mourning Modernism: Literature, Catastrophe, and the Politics of Consolation* (Fordham University Press, 2011), 53.

[26] Virginia Woolf, *Between the Acts*, ed. Mark Hussey (Cambridge University Press, 2011), 31–2.

[27] Woolf, *Complete Shorter Fiction*, 281 and 282.

Stef Craps.[28] His ignorance is spectacular. Everybody knows about Angela, "even Sissy Miller," who admits B. M. was her brother. The reader is no exception, and "The Legacy" is an exercise in dramatic irony: in the second paragraph, for example, Gilbert thinks, "Yes, [...] it was strange that Angela had left everything in such order," and then does not speculate further (281). The diary is close to stream-of-consciousness, censored only so far as to protect against definitive accusations. For example, the suicide of her lover is noted in: "He threatened that if I did not..." (286). One could argue that Gilbert has access to her thoughts, that the diary provides him with the opportunity to enter her mind. He even attempts an act of sympathetic imagination, much like Clarissa: "He could see her in front of him. She was standing on the kerb in Piccadilly. Her eyes stared; her fists were clenched. Here came the car..." (287). Again, the problem is vantage. He is imagining what it would be like to watch her, not what it would be like to *be* her. The experience produces no insight into her character. The second ellipsis is used not to protect information but to avoid knowledge. He can imagine her death, but only so far, and the revelations come too late to offer true intimacy. Like any suicide note, this is a monologue that precludes the possibility of dialogue. The fifteen green leather volumes are an ironic legacy, a testament of death, a tragic counterpoint to the child the couple never had.

The most remarkable feature of Rhoda's suicide in *The Waves* (1931) is the scant attention it receives from the novel. Rhoda telegraphs her death from the beginning: on her first night at school, away from home, she says, "Here I am nobody. I have no face."[29] When her friend Percival dies, she vows, "I will go [...] I will make a pilgrimage [...] I will fling myself fearlessly into trams, into omnibuses" (129). A late monologue begins, "Oh, life, how I have dreaded you" (162). It therefore comes as a shock to the reader when Bernard emerges swinging his stick from his hairdresser, and

> evoked to serve as opposite to myself the figure of Rhoda, always so furtive, always with fear in her eyes, always seeking some pillar in the desert, to find which she had gone; she had killed herself. "Wait," I said, putting my arm in imagination (thus we consort with our friends) through her arm. "Wait until these omnibuses have gone by. Do not cross so dangerously. These men are your brothers." In persuading her I was also persuading my own soul.
>
> (225)

[28] Stef Craps, "Virginia Woolf: 'Kew Gardens' and 'The Legacy,'" in *A Companion to the British and Irish Short Story*, ed. Cheryl Alexander Malcolm and David Malcolm (Wiley-Blackwell, 2008), 199.

[29] Virginia Woolf, *The Waves*, ed. Michael Herbert and Susan Sellers (Cambridge University Press, 2011), 25. All subsequent references are noted parenthetically in the text.

Several pages later, he says, "I see far away, quivering like a gold thread, the pillar Rhoda saw, and feel the rush of the wind of her flight when she leapt" (231).

The passage has prompted strong reactions. Garrett Stewart, who calls it "[d]ying by elision," writes that Rhoda "leaves the novel as the most extravagant avatar of discontinuity in modern fiction,"[30] Annette Oxidine that hers is "one of the eeriest suicides in modern fiction—eerie because Rhoda disappears from the novel instead of dying 'in' it."[31] Without narration to contextualize, clarify, and voice internal thoughts, the death of Rhoda is second-hand, below-the-fold news, buried halfway into the paragraph. It is only on rereading that we realize an earlier reference to her "leav[ing] us, flying past us to the desert" was in fact the first mention of her suicide (213). The use of past perfect ("she had killed herself") is a further indignity. *The Waves* is written almost exclusively in the present tense, but Rhoda's death has already happened by the time we read about it. The formal innovations that distinguish the novel—the near-exclusive reliance on speech, the diffusion of a central narrative through an unwieldy number of characters—coalesce here into the report of a suicide from an unreliable narrator who is using the victim as a reflection of himself. By the end of the paragraph, he will be doing the same with the rest of his friends: "Nor do I always know if I am [...] Bernard or Neville, Louis, Susan, Jinny or Rhoda" (225). Her suicide, it seems, is evocative for Bernard, the details, unimportant. The psychological and even circumstantial details of her death, no doubt of interest to many readers, are left to our imagination. The "conspiracy of silence and willed ignorance" has been observed.[32]

There is one precedent for Septimus Warren Smith. In 1903, when she was still Virginia Stephen, Woolf read an account of a woman who drowned herself in the Serpentine, the artificial lake that connects Hyde Park and Kensington Gardens. The woman left a note that read, in part, "No father, no mother, no work."[33] In her journal, Woolf considers the meaning of the note ("She had learnt perhaps the self respect & purity that come from work") and imagines the scene of her death ("Then slipping off the weight that had been too much

[30] Quoted in Annette Oxindine, "Rhoda Submerged: Lesbian Suicide in *The Waves*," in *Virginia Woolf: Lesbian Readings*, ed. Eileen Barrett and Patricia Cramer (New York University Press, 1997), 215–16.

[31] Oxindine, "Rhoda Submerged," 203.

[32] Alan Warren Friedman, *Fictional Death and the Modernist Enterprise* (Cambridge University Press, 1995), 61.

[33] Virginia Woolf, *A Passionate Apprentice: The Early Journals 1897–1909*, ed. Mitchell A. Leaska (Harcourt Brace Jovanovich, 1990), 211.

for her, she sank into the waters").[34] In one passage, without the use of quotation marks, she shifts from third to first person: "But her husband leaves her for some other woman, & her children die, or desert her. Then of a sudden comes that pang—Without husband or children, I yet had parents. If they were alive now I should not be alone. Whatever my sin my father & mother would have given me protection & comfort."[35] This empathetic gesture, this attempt to imagine Andrew Bennett's "lived experience" of a suicide, would remain dormant for over twenty years.[36]

Mrs. Dalloway

The two scenes in *Mrs. Dalloway* are worth quoting at length. Suffering from shell shock, grieving the death of a beloved comrade, and under poor psychiatric care, Septimus chooses death:

> There remained only the window, the large Bloomsbury-lodging house window; the tiresome, the troublesome, and rather melodramatic business of opening the window and throwing himself out. It was their idea of tragedy, not his or Rezia's (for she was with him). Holmes and Bradshaw like that sort of thing. (He sat on the sill.) But he would wait till the very last moment. He did not want to die. Life was good. The sun hot. Only human beings? Coming down the staircase opposite an old man stopped and stared at him. Holmes was at the door. "I'll give it you!" he cried, and flung himself vigorously, violently down on to Mrs. Filmer's area railings.
>
> (133–4)

One of his doctors, Sir William Bradshaw, later attends Clarrisa's party, and his wife shares the news with their hostess:

> "A young man (that is what Sir William is telling Mr. Dalloway) had killed himself. He had been in the army." [...] He had killed himself—but how? Always her body went through it, when she was told, first, suddenly, of an accident; her dress flamed, her body burnt. He had thrown himself from a window. Up had flashed the ground; through him, blundering, bruising, went the rusty spikes. There he lay with a thud, thud, thud in his brain, and then a suffocation of blackness. So she saw it. But why had he done it? [...] Death was defiance. Death

[34] Woolf, *A Passionate Apprentice*, 213.
[35] Woolf, *A Passionate Apprentice*, 212.
[36] Andrew Bennett, *Suicide Century: Literature and Suicide from James Joyce to David Foster Wallace* (Cambridge University Press, 2017), 4.

> was an attempt to communicate, people feeling the impossibility of reaching the centre which, mystically, evaded them; closeness drew apart; rapture faded; one was alone. There was an embrace in death [...] Somehow it was her disaster—her disgrace [...] She felt somehow very like him—the young man who had killed himself. She felt glad that he had done it; thrown it away [...] He made her feel the beauty; made her feel the fun. But she must go back. She must assemble. And she came in from the little room.
>
> (164–7)[37]

Critics are divided on the second scene, but they have tended toward suspicion. For Hite, "Septimus's extreme suffering is hardly comparable to Clarissa's empathetic 'disgrace' at hearing of his suicide." In the cruel tradition of her class, "it is as though she can let the lower orders do her dying for her."[38] Karen DeMeester objects not to her reaction but her subsequent actions: "Clarissa silences Septimus and robs his death of meaning by refusing to change in response to his message."[39] Trudi Tate warns the reader against "replicating her romanticization of Septimus's death,"[40] and Deborah Guth argues that "her quasi-mystical interpretation in no way reflects Septimus' own experience." Instead, his death is a "ritual sacrifice—the sacrifice of an individual reality in favor of the vision."[41] There are credulous readings, too. Laura Sager, for example, writes, "Death is transformed from the ultimate separation into the ultimate union, the most complete form of embrace,"[42] while Elizabeth Abel reads the scene as "a cathartic, vicarious experience of death that releases her to experience life's pleasures more intensely."[43]

The textual evidence, like the tonal, is ambiguous. Still, in her characterization of Clarissa and in her evocation of London and its network of intersecting lives, Woolf prepares the reader to view the epiphany as authentic, or at least plausible. Both narrator and characters conceive of themselves through metaphors of connection, and these connections are sustained by direct and indirect contact. When Richard Dalloway and Hugh Whitbread leave Lady Bruton, they remain

37 The lines "He made her feel the beauty; made her feel the fun" are only in the American edition of the novel.

38 Hite, *Woolf's Ambiguities*, 11.

39 Karen DeMeester, "Trauma and Recovery in Virginia Woolf's *Mrs. Dalloway*," *Modern Fiction Studies* 44, no. 3 (Fall 1998), 663.

40 Trudi Tate, "Mrs. Dalloway and the Armenian Question," *Textual Practice* 8, no. 3 (1994), 479.

41 Deborah Guth, "Rituals of Self-Deception: Clarissa Dalloway's Final Moment of Vision," *Twentieth Century Literature* 36, no. 1 (Spring 1990), 36, 39.

42 Laura Sager, "Septimus' Suicide," *Virginia Woolf Bulletin*, no. 3 (January 2000), 27.

43 Elizabeth Abel, *Virginia Woolf and the Fictions of Psychoanalysis* (The University of Chicago Press, 1993), 38.

"attached to her by a thin thread [...] which would stretch and stretch, get thinner and thinner as they walked across London" (101). Richard's mind then drifts to Clarissa "as a single spider's [...] attaches itself to the point of a leaf" (103). He is "eager, yes, very eager, to travel that spider's thread of attachment between himself and Clarissa," so he buys her roses. Their thread is strong, and the coincidence of their spontaneous purchase of flowers is an example of the kind of telepathy she will later experience with Septimus. Clarissa chooses a different metaphor: reflecting on her eventual death, she is comforted that

> somehow in the streets of London, on the ebb and flow of things, here, there, she survived, Peter survived, lived in each other, she being part [...] of people she had never met; being laid out like a mist between the people she knew best, who lifted her on their branches as she had seen the trees lift the mist, but it spread ever so far, her life, herself (8).

Both Richard and Clarissa extend their influence throughout London, but her mist is more indiscriminate than his threading; its potential to affect strangers better supports Clarissa's belief that she has been transformed through indirect contact with Septimus. Rezia, listening to a poor old woman sing, combines the two metaphors: "Cheerfully, almost gaily, the invincible thread of sound wound up into the air like the smoke from a cottage chimney, winding up clean beech trees and issuing in a tuft of blue smoke among the topmost leaves" (74).

Clarissa, in particular, is attuned to these smoke signs. When she leaves to buy the flowers, the narrator writes, "Her only gift was knowing people almost by instinct, she thought" (8). *She thought* might be a concession to doubt, but *only* suggests it is one to modesty. Clarissa has few talents, but one is her empathy. The thought is soon validated. She meets Peter Walsh, whom she hasn't seen in five years, and she guesses he will find her grown older. He does but says nothing; only the reader knows Clarissa is correct. Peter admits that "she was very shrewd—a far better judge of character than Sally" (68) and remembers the "odd affinities she had with people she had never spoken to, some woman in the street, some man behind a counter" (136). When Peter is squirming at her party, Clarissa notices his discomfort and reassures him with the economy of a hostess who has to attend to a number of guests: "We will talk later" (160). Peter in fact begrudges Clarissa her empathy: she has double her husband's wits and yet still "had to see things through his eyes" (69). She is seated at the center of Richard's mind. Despite the condescension some of the characters, and even the author, exhibit toward Clarissa, hers is a true and humanizing gift.[44] When she describes her parties as an "offering," an opportunity to "to combine, to create," she sounds more like an artist mixing paints than a socialite trying to impress the wealthy and the powerful (109).

Peter annoys Clarissa precisely because he fails to empathize as she does; he doesn't have "the ghost of a notion what any one else was feeling" (42). This contrast is illustrated through their respective reactions to Septimus. Peter overlaps with him twice. The first time, in Regent's Park, he sees Septimus with Rezia, perceives something is wrong between them, then universalizes their situation: "And that is being young [...] To be having an awful scene" (64). This uncorks a stream of thought that ends with a nationalistic paean: "Never had he seen London look so enchanting [...] the richness; the greenness; the civilization, after India." Clarissa, he knows, would have looked closer, "she would have talked to those lovers, if she had thought them unhappy" (64). She would have learned that their problems are in fact more dire than those of "lovers squabbling under a tree." Rezia has just told Septimus, "I am so unhappy," and Septimus is smiling because he is hallucinating Evans, his dead comrade, emerging unwounded from the bushes—a symptom of his shell shock. Civilization and its expression through the Great War and medical malpractice are responsible for this hallucination, this unhappiness. London is more like India than Peter realizes. The second time he overlaps with Septimus, Peter hears the "light high bell of the ambulance" sent to retrieve his corpse (135). Again, he turns to celebration: "One of the triumphs of civilisation [...] Swiftly, cleanly, the ambulance sped to the hospital, having picked up instantly, humanely, some poor devil; some one hit on the head, struck down by disease, knocked over perhaps a minute or so ago at one of these crossings, as might happen to oneself." The series of adjectives before the semicolon (*swiftly*, *cleanly*, *instantly*, *humanely*) are so enthusiastic they are comical, while the speculations about the cause of death all make Septimus the object of the sentence, the passive victim of chance. In truth, Peter's *triumph*, the ambulance, is only summoned because civilization has made it necessary. Peter, who would be familiar with colonial propaganda, is praising England for her swift, clean, instant, and humane treatment of the wounds she creates. His ultimate sympathy is not with the victim "stretched on a shelf with a doctor and nurse" but with the passersby who thinks "how easily it might have been them there," a warped variation on Clarissa's empathy.

[44] Woolf admits, in response to a critical remark from Lytton Strachey, "I found Clarissa in some way tinselly [...] I think some distance for her persisted." Woolf, *Diary Three*, 32.

Clarissa has no reason to believe she is "somehow very like" Septimus, but the reader does. For example, there is the structural echo of their introductions. The two first lines of the novel, "Mrs. Dalloway said she would buy the flowers herself. For Lucy had her work cut out for her," are enjambed; the lines cross two paragraphs (3). The first two lines about Septimus are likewise interrupted by a paragraph break: "Septimus Warren Smith, who found himself unable to pass, heard him. Septimus Warren Smith, aged about thirty, pale-faced, beak-nosed, wearing brown shoes and a shabby overcoat[...]" (13). The stuttered repetition of his full name, the second sentence that seems unaware of the first, both are awkward choices that mimic his arrested experience of time, the traumatic loop that keeps Evans alive and Rezia distant. Like Septimus, Clarissa has a semi-invisible illness: she is recovering from the Spanish flu. Each sits under the Sword of Damocles in the form of a relapse. At the end of the novel, there is another structural echo: an old man stops and stares at Septimus before he jumps, and Clarissa observes an old woman, in the room opposite, before she returns to her party. Is each of these details red herrings, and is the reader expected to dismiss them all with cynicism?

Without a doubt, there is evidence to support a suspicious reading of Clarissa's epiphany. It is not difficult to make the case that the wife of a member of parliament and hostess to the prime minister of the United Kingdom—one who does not know the difference between Armenians and Albanians—has little or no insight into the psychological consequences of combat. Before the party, Clarissa acknowledges the limitations of even the closest interpersonal connections. Sounding a little like her author, she thinks about the "solitude" in people, how "even between husband and wife [there is] a gulf" (107). In contrast to her earlier thoughts, she regrets that after her death, "no one in the whole world would know how she had loved it all" (110). Paragraphs before the novel ends, Woolf gives the idea pride of place. Sally, waiting to speak to Clarissa, asks Peter, "[W]hat can one know even of the people one lives with every day? [...] Are we not all prisoners?" (172). Another metaphor, this one in sharp distinction to Richard's threads and Clarissa's mist. Furthermore, when she hears of the suicide, Clarissa uses the polite euphemism *accident*, as if Septimus were standing still and the railings hit him. Moreover, if her body *always* "went through it first," her reaction in this case is not unique; it is her established response to tragedy. She also adds the detail of the crucifixion by "rusty spikes," a little sensational and perhaps the reason Hite calls him "the sacrificial victim of her midlife crisis."[45] Finally, the semi-biblical structure of the sentences, which begin with prepositions (*up*, *through*) and adverbs (*there*, *so*), are difficult to read without irony, in particular, "So she saw it." Surely "She saw it" would suffice. At the risk of being literal: no, she did not.

Even so, the narrator does not describe the moments between Septimus's leap and his death, a silence Woolf observes despite her otherwise-complete description of his suicide. We cannot compare it with Clarissa's for accuracy. Be that as it may, there are clues that point to their genuine relationship as secret sharers. Her physical reaction to the news of an accident ("her dress flamed, her body burnt") has no literal connection to his death, but Septimus uses the word *flame* and its derivatives seven times throughout the novel, and in the last, he uses both *flames* and *burnt*: "Miracles, revelations, agonies, loneliness, falling through the sea, down, down into the flames, all were burnt out" (126). Her "quasi-mystical interpretation" ("people feeling the impossibility of reaching the centre which, mystically, evaded them; closeness drew apart; rapture faded, one was alone") is an imperfect reproduction of his philosophy, but Clarissa is working in the same apocalyptic genre and with the same metaphorical language. Her reading of his suicide, "Death was a defiance," is consistent with Septimus framing his struggle as a battle between us (he and Rezia) and them (his doctors). While it is unclear whether his last words, "I'll give it you!" are a concession to "their idea of tragedy" or a defiant coda to his relationship with Sir William, her feelings about the doctor seems to align Clarissa "with him," not them. When she meets him, she senses something beneath the veneer: "one wouldn't like Sir William to see one unhappy. No; not that man" (163).

Where does this leave the reader? That depends upon a line at the end of Clarissa's reverie. Hite registers her objections through direct quotation with added punctuation and emphasis: "Made her feel the beauty? Made her feel the *fun*?"[46] Bethea writes, "If this is all that a man's death can achieve, however—a transient moment of 'fun'—the impoverishment of *Mrs. Dalloway*'s world is clear."[47] Neither indicates they are discussing an elliptical sentence. In other words, Septimus's death made her feel the fun *of what*? The thought prompts Clarissa's return to the party, to Peter and Sally, those with whom, apart from Richard, she is closest, even if time has frayed their connections. It seems reasonable to

45 Hite, *Woolf's Ambiguities*, 13.

46 Hite, *Woolf's Ambiguities*, 11.

47 Arthur F. Bethea, "Septimus Smith, the War-Shattered Christ Substitute in *Mrs. Dalloway*," *The Explicator* 68, no. 4 (2010), 251.

assume the referent is life. For Clarissa, it is a lark, a plunge, and no one will know how she loved it all. She has heard, and she embodies, the most important point of Septimus's suicide, "Life is good." His death is not, as Jeffrey Berman argues, "an attempt to communicate" that "forever shatters communication."[48] Nor has communication been "diminished by a gap in meaning that to an extent exists in all attempts to communicate," as DeMeester claims.[49] This better describes the suicides of Rhoda and Angela Clandon. Bethea's argument about the transience of the fun and DeMeester's about Clarissa "refusing to change in response to his message" rely on speculation about her actions after the novel is over. In the present, on Wednesday, June 13, 1923, Clarissa hears about his death and returns to the duties and pleasures of life. What better response to his message? When Evans dies, Septimus congratulates himself for feeling "very little and very reasonably" (77). Later, he comes to believe that "human nature had condemned him to death" because "he did not feel" (81–2). Clarissa, who knows people almost by instinct, who has odd affinities with strangers, is the ideal organ for his message. "I meant to write about death," Woolf wrote in her diary around this time, "only life came breaking in as usual."[50]

"The sun hot." The line follows "Life was good," and it is an echo of song from *Cymbeline* (1611). Its opening lines and refrain, "Fear no more the heat o' the sun," run through the minds of both characters throughout *Mrs. Dalloway* (for Clarissa, 8, 27, 36, and 166; for Septimus, 125). In *Cymbeline*, the song is a dirge for a woman disguised as a boy, sung by her brothers who believe she (or rather, he) is a stranger. The sun is an anguished symbol, representing both the source of life and the source of its misery. The dramatic irony, the mix of pathos and humor, all create a tension around genre, a tonal ambiguity. The encounter between Clarissa and Septimus, threaded by this allusion to Shakespeare, encompasses a similar breadth of ambiguous meaning. It is preposterous, and it is sincere. Septimus's suicide is a rejection of life that affirms life's value.

The evidence therefore seems to suggest that Woolf, at least, viewed Clarissa's epiphany as sincere, which makes the scene a vindication of her method: if Clarissa can "share something" with Septimus, then so can we. Steam-of-consciousness provides Woolf with the means to enter the lives of others, to perform an empathetic occupation of the mind that is impossible in the bounds of real life. The choice to select a suicidal subject is atypical in her work and in

[48] Jeffrey Berman, *Surviving Literary Suicide* (University of Massachusetts Press, 1999), 90.

[49] DeMeester, "Trauma and Recovery in Virginia Woolf's *Mrs. Dalloway*," 665.

[50] Woolf, *Diary Two*, 167.

the modernist canon in general. Each approach has its strengths and limitations. There is a humility to *The Waves*, an acknowledgment of the epistemological limitations on the witness of a suicide. Still, it does little to engage with the victim or their story; it is in essence an act of surrender. On the other hand, there is a humanity to *Mrs. Dalloway* and its fraught but honest attempt to use the formal tools of a modern novelist to engage with a suicidal mind. Nevertheless, ignoring the epistemological limitations risks an appeal to mysticism and belief in an implausible shared experience across class and gender lines by two people who never meet and have very different relationships to death. Tate warns us against replicating Clarissa's "romanticization of Septimus's death," but it would be more accurate to describe the romanticization as Woolf's. Perhaps it is worth noting that a similar logic animates her suicide note. She affirms the value of her life with Leonard ("You have given me the greatest possible happiness") and conceives of her death as an affirmation of his life ("I know that I am spoiling your life, that without me you could work. And you will I know").[51] She was wrong.

Woolf observed the "conspiracy of silence" that characterizes so many modernist depictions of suicide, except once. *Mrs. Dalloway* is the counterpoint, an epistemological success. The method is much the same as in Marie Corelli and Robert Louis Stevenson, with stream-of-consciousness substituting for the suicide note. Once again, it is the effects, rather than the causes, that are under debate, but unlike her predecessors, Woolf is unconcerned with punishment, either legal or divine. She is instead interested in the interpersonal effects of suicide, on the mist it creates and how it spreads. Whether Septimus, like Mrs. Brown, "slip[s] through" her fingers is a decision left to each reader, likely determined by one's faith in the imagination to represent the minds of others. For the cynical, the speech that replaces silence has no truth value; it is a distinction without a difference. For Woolf, the problem of consciousness, in her letters, her diary, and her published nonfiction, never held such prominence again. She was right, it seems, to blame her age. Toward the end of the drafting of *Mrs. Dalloway*, she wrote in her diary, "Being at a low ebb with my book—the death of Septimus,—I begin to count myself a failure."[52] At some point, she settled her doubts. Following the publication of *The Years* (1937), recovering from her usual

[51] Virginia Woolf, *The Letters of Virginia Woolf Volume Six: 1936–1941*, ed. Nigel Nicolson and Joanne Trautmann (Harcourt Brace Jovanovich, 1980), 481.

[52] Woolf, *Diary Two*, 307–8.

postpartum depression, Woolf describes the process as a balm rather than an obstacle: "A curiously physical sense; as if one had been living in another body, which is removed, & all that living is ended. As usual, the remedy is to enter other lives, I suppose."[53] By this point, the process warranted mourning of its death and celebration of its birth.

[53] Virginia Woolf, *The Diary of Virginia Woolf Volume Five: 1936–1941*, ed. Anne Olivier Bell (Harvest, 1984), 105.

5

The Suicidal Type: The Sociology of Suicide, Golden Age Detective Fiction, and the Problem of Causality

While vacationing in Pendlebury, Inspector Mallett passes an evening with Leonard Dickinson. Leonard is a morose eccentric who is compiling a collection of pessimistic aphorisms for a homemade calendar, and he soon launches into a depressive rant: "We have this advantage over the snail—we can make our trail end when and where we wish."[1] Leonard's body is found the following morning, and a note is left behind that reads, "*We are in the power of no calamity, while Death is in our own*" (20; emphasis in original). This is Thomas Browne, who coined the word *suicide*, but this is also a detective novel, and when a suicide clause is found in Leonard's will, his son begins to have doubts: "Can you imagine a man who really contemplated suicide devoting years of his life to selecting and arranging the three hundred and sixty-five gloomiest observations on life that he could find?" (60). His sister agrees: "Father didn't kill himself [...] I know *because* I know [...] He just wasn't that sort of person" (39; emphasis in original). Near the end of the novel, the final case is made by the family lawyer: "From my knowledge of him, I should not say that he would have committed suicide—in the first year of a life policy, at any rate. He knew that much about insurance, I have no doubt" (179). Furthermore, on the night of the supposed suicide, Leonard left out an apple for the following morning: "Not a likely thing for a man to do if he knew he wasn't going to be alive to eat it, was it?" (64). Inspector Mallett, both witness and investigator, has his suspicions from the beginning: "People who contemplated such things didn't confide their intentions, whether to chance acquaintances or to anybody else" (16).

1 Cyril Hare, *Suicide Excepted* (Perennial Library, 1983), 12. All subsequent references are noted parenthetically in the text.

Thus, in Cyril Hare's *Suicide Excepted* (1939), those who knew Leonard Dickinson best have no trouble determining that he could not have killed himself. The equation runs something like this: his character + the insurance policy + the apple = foul play. Each of the witnesses eliminates suicide by citing generalizations as rules: a man who does this, or a man who does that, is not a man who kills himself. Hare vindicates them all. Leonard, of course, was murdered. The detective story, which generally requires the perpetrator and victim to be different people, has little time for suicide. Detectives want to know *who* is responsible for a crime, and they answer this question by investigating *why* they are responsible—the motivation of the perpetrator is a means to uncovering their identity. In the case of a suicide, the identity of the perpetrator is obvious, and their bodies prove legible to most witnesses: son, sister, and lawyer all correctly read this clue. "That's the one advantage of suicide," says a character in Margery Allingham's *The Fashion in Shrouds* (1938), "everyone knows who did it."[2] The typical substance of the drama, their motives, is likewise apparent, and therefore detection is unnecessary. Apart from villains who want to avoid punishment, suicide is rare in Golden Age detective fiction. Voluntary death does not provide a suitable puzzle for a Hercule Poirot or a Lord Peter Wimsey.

The question of the suicidal type, of what kind of man or woman *does* kill themselves, would dominate much of the discourse around suicide in the twentieth century, especially after the sociologist Émile Durkheim's landmark monograph, *Suicide* (1897). Durkheim and his contemporaries were interested in correlation, not causation. He argues, for example, that Protestants commit suicide more than Catholics, the old more than the young. When applied to individual cases, each correlation nonetheless contains an implied question of causation: did he kill himself, at least in part, because he was a Protestant? Did she because she was old? Durkheim refuses to supplement his analysis with nonsocial causes, in particular psychological causes. This is not because they are irrelevant but because they are immeasurable. Consequently, the problem of causality rests uneasily in his work. No such qualms can be found in detective fiction, the genre readiest to adopt sociological readings of suicide. In the following chapter, I will argue that writers such as Hare, Agatha Christie, and Dorothy L. Sayers all endorsed the model of the suicidal type constructed by the early suicidologists with greater readiness and fewer qualifications than its

[2] Margery Allinghan, *The Fashion in Shrouds* (Manor Books, 1976), 38.

progenitors. Because these writers abandon the distinction between correlation and causation, reducing suicides into a series of signals or clues, they free the sociological portrait of its central explanatory failure.

Durkheim's Predecessors: Morselli, Westcott, and Strahan

First, a suicidological review is in order. Medical discourse around suicide accelerated at the end of the nineteenth century. By one estimate, there were already four thousand works on the subject by 1897.[3] Jean Baechler divides these works into two theoretical categories, sociological and psychological.[4] Margaret Pabst Battin, editor of the mammoth *The Ethics of Suicide: Historical Sources* (2015), likewise identifies the "full force [… of] the time of Freud and Durkheim" as the key "transition […] from the conception of suicide as a sin and a crime to the conception of it as the product of psychological and social forces beyond an individual's control."[5] The publication of Enrico Morselli's *Suicide: An Essay on Comparative Moral Statistics* (1881; revised and translated into English 1882) was a flashpoint in the new science of suicide. Morselli anticipates Durkheim in his methodological handling of suicide data and his advocacy for the explanatory power of "moral statistics." A professor and asylum physician-in-chief, he was among the first to take suicide, which was previously under the purview of religion and philosophy, into that of science. From the beginning, Andrew Bennett's "lived experience […] of suicide," is exiled.[6] Morselli admits that "dealing here with the inward phenomena of conscience, statistics cannot presume to learn the true mental state or psychical movement which has preceded the act of suicide; it is necessary to limit ourselves to an approximation" (7). He must "stop short" at the "sensible phases" of the "human conscience" (8). Still, he is unconvinced that this problem is prohibitive: "with the laws that regulate social organism[s], the individualism of human activities disappears, as in a most complicated piece of mechanism the movement of one single wheel constitutes a small part of the whole work" (10). Generalizations determine behavior rather than the other way around, and selecting a legal

3 Whitney Pope, *Durkheim's Suicide: A Classic Analyzed* (University of Chicago Press, 1976), 4.

4 Jean Baechler, *Suicides*, trans. Barry Cooper (Basil Blackwell, 1979), 6.

5 Margaret Pabst Battin, ed., *The Ethics of Suicide: Historical Sources* (Oxford University Press, 2015), 476.

6 Andrew Bennett, *Suicide Century: Literature and Suicide from James Joyce to David Foster Wallace* (Cambridge University Press, 2017), 4.

metaphor enables him to assume the authority of language that is derived from abstractions and imposed from above. Under these laws, "individual will becomes absorbed by the general will" (187) and spontaneity is repressed by the "really wonderful regularity of social phenomena" (255). The hard problem of consciousness is resolved with an appeal to instinct: "the psychical life of the individual is but the reflex of the nature and characteristics of that social aggregate in the midst of which it thinks, wills, and acts" (114). Note that his use of *it* rather than *he* or *she* indicates that he attributes thinking, willing, and acting to "the psychical life" rather than "the individual," to the function rather than the human being performing that function.

Morselli viewed humanity—or, as he calls us early in the text, "living and operating numbers" (3)—as a constant. Just as the mixing of cyanide and sulfate will always yield the same result in chemistry, so too will any given combination of biological, social, and geographical factors in the human (188). As an exercise in considering the limitations of this approach, imagine two men of the same age, nationality, religion, marital status, income, and profession. If both were to commit suicide, how much would these shared characteristics tell you? How much would they leave out? The problem is not that Morselli takes as his object of study social causes. It is that he denies the value of nonsocial ones. The whole spectrum of human experience is limited to this kind of macro-reductionism or aggregate blindness, in which sociological concerns eclipse psychological ones and free will becomes nonexistent. I am not sure, as Bennett is, that suicide "fundamentally resists the *socio*," but it certainly does not rely exclusively on the *socio* for explanation (51; emphasis in original). Morselli is fond of the phrase *paying tribute*, as in "every year [...] humanity must pay a tribute of new victims [... to] the tide of suicide" (275). An apt metaphor of chance and obligation for a species that has little control over whether it drowns. It appears nineteen times in his book.[7] Only in this appeal to mysticism does he concede to the unknown, and he can only do so through the use of metaphor. This is not, after all, what the language of science was built for. Even so, the bugle call of *Suicide* is unmistakable: "To science alone will belong in future the functions of regulator and moderator of public morals" (372). For Morselli, voluntary death belongs to science, and psychology is not a science.

[7] 23, 47, 54, 92, 193, 212, 245, two on 249, 256, 271, 290, 292, 297, 298, 304, 362, and 364. I know of one occasion where Durkheim uses the same metaphor: 338. He also refers to suicide as a "tax" (342), a "debt" (360), and a "destiny" (361). All subsequent references are noted parenthetically in the text.

The London coroner William Wynn Westcott followed Morselli with *Suicide: Its History, Literature, Jurisprudence, Causation, and Prevention* (1885), the first full-length, English-language study of the subject since Forbes Winslow's *The Anatomy of Suicide* (1840). Westcott's position is "scientific" as opposed to "Ethical," and he proposes treating the causes of suicide "in a manner similar to that which is ordinarily pursued with regard to diseases."[8] The comparison suggests that madness and suicide are phenomena that invade rather than originate in the individual. Westcott even appropriates Morselli's metaphor of the chemist "combining his elements [… to] prepare a new body," and so, for example, the combination of two races yields a suicide rate that is "intermediate between them" (76). His cure is panoptic, both "a constant watchfulness" (173) and "the immediate removal from society of any person […] who shows any tendency to self-destruction" (168). For Westcott, the problem is not to treat the suicidal subject so that they no longer contemplate suicide but to quarantine them so that society is unaffected by their deaths and demeanor. His stern approach can occasionally yield ludicrous analyses: at the end of a section on morality, Westcott writes a one-sentence paragraph—"In 'Aurora Floyd' and 'Lady Audley's Secret', two novels of high standing, suicide is suggested definitely as a remedy for trouble, at least twelve times"—as if context and tone were irrelevant, the number twelve weighty enough to blot out such literary concerns (92).

The physician and barrister S. A. K. Strahan provides a key theoretical precedent to Durkheim in *Suicide and Insanity* (1893). For Strahan, there are "two great classes" of voluntary death, the *rational* or *quasi-suicide* and the *irrational* or *true suicide*.[9] The rational suicide is committed when "death is deliberately chosen and embraced by a rational being, as for some reason preferable to life" (34). These fall under two categories: those who die for gain and those who die to escape evil. Irrational suicides, on the other hand, "are impelled to destroy their lives when insane [… or] give way to a sudden impulse [when sane]" (65). Strahan argues that ancient suicides tended to be rational, modern ones irrational. Crude as this configuration may be—how, for example, would he classify a suicide committed to escape evil that is nonetheless the product of "a sudden impulse"?—it is a comprehensive and scientific system of classifying

[8] Wynn Westcott, *Suicide: Its History, Literature, Jurisprudence, Causation, and Prevention* (H. K. Lewis, 1885), 6, 65. All subsequent references are noted parenthetically in the text.

[9] S. A. K. Strahan, *Suicide and Insanity* (Swan Sonnenschein and Co., 1893), 32. All subsequent references are noted parenthetically in the text.

voluntary death. Note that Strahan reserves the name *true* for the suicide whose behavior is more inscrutable, those whose causes are psychological, not social. Suicides that are rational are given the qualifier *quasi*. His language betrays the truth: the causes of a true suicide are beyond his means of knowledge building.

Perhaps influenced by Max Nordau's *Degeneration* (1892; translated into English 1895), Strahan attributes a rise in "the acquired predisposition" toward irrational suicide to the advance of civilization (148). Under "natural conditions," the predisposed "would promptly perish," for the "absence of this fundamental instinct (of self-preservation) is *per se* irrefragable proof of unfitness to live" (30). Suicide is "merely one of the eliminative processes of natural selection." For Strahan, there is an ethical quality to this kind of death—it is a tonic for the species. Since civilization has interrupted such Darwinian suicides, these "markedly degenerate peoples [...] deteriorating with every generation" (15) are "permitted and at times even induced to contaminate the race by the propagation of their unfitness" (69–70). Suicide is like hemophilia, and its treatment is eugenic: each family should "increase its vitality by attention to the laws of health, and by the infusion of fresh and untainted blood" (91). Those who are "markedly unfit to propagate their kind [... should not] be allowed to contaminate the race and increase suffering and misery by propagating his or her unfitness" (79). With no Swiftian irony, Strahan encourages us to adopt the attitude of "men who spend thousands of pounds yearly in improving the breed of their horses and dogs, who understand the laws of heredity, and would not breed even a pig from other than a good stock" (82). Whereas Westcott proposes excluding the suicidal from society, Strahan wants to exclude them from genealogy. In addition to those of disease and livestock, he also uses the metaphor "breakdowns of the machine" (159). Malfunctions can be identified, and machines can be fixed or scrapped.

As for the causes of breakdowns, Strahan admits that it is "absolutely impossible accurately to classify suicides as to the causes which prompt them to the act" (63). This is a dismissal masked as an explanation. After all, much of his book implies causes: race, climate, religion, sex, age, etc. Strahan writes that modern suicides are "due to madness, disgust of life, and last and greatest, that uncontrollable impulse to death which cannot be explained," an admission that appears to undermine his entire project (15). If the "last and greatest" cause cannot be explained under the framework of suicidology, shouldn't that framework be altered, reassessed, or at least integrate this failure into its conclusions? Over and over again, Strahan concedes his limitations and then moves on. In his chapter "Suicide and Insanity," for example, he writes, "It is certain we shall never discover a means of getting to know the mental state of the suicide just anterior to his fatal act. It would seem impossible that we can ever arrive at the stage where reliable statistics on the subject might be obtainable, and it is clear that all existing statistics relative to the question are valueless" (92). In the next, "The Suicidal Impulse," he writes that the notion of an *impulse* is usually dismissed in cases where the criminal remains alive because of "the impossibility of proving on independent evidence, the existence of such irresistible impulse in any given case" (121). It is appropriate with a suicide because "such [a] decision can injure no one" (121). The difference is not in truth value but in legal practicalities: the silence of the suicide allows Strahan to impose an explanation where the speech of the living criminal would prohibit it. Later, he cautions that "above all things," one should avoid the "dangerous" practice of "bringing charges of doubtful veracity [...] against the dead, who cannot reply" (179–80). He does not take his own advice.

In one Oxford undergraduate, at least, Strahan finds an ideal case study. Before shooting himself in his rooms, the young man wrote, "The reason of my committing this act may, perhaps, seem incomprehensible, but I suppose it is chiefly that my morbid desire for death from my childhood has grown too strong for me. It may be madness, but I fear not." Almost approving, Strahan adds, "The letter was rational, clear, logical, and sympathetic" (129). The causes are nonsocial but the result is the elimination of a broken machine. And like Leonard Dickinson, this student can be reduced to a mathematical equation: his character + a mounting, morbid desire for death = an irrational—or *true*—suicide.

Durkheim

Durkheim's thesis in *Suicide*, derived from the 26,000 cases he classified with the help of his nephew, Marcel Mauss, is this: both a strong presence and a strong absence of either social integration or social regulation precipitate the choice of death. Each suicide falls into one of four categories. The first is the *egotistical suicide*, or suicide by "excessive individualism" (225). Because he has failed to integrate with society, because he is estranged from family and the community at large, an egotistical suicide loses the sense that his actions have purpose. Werther, most certainly, was an egotistical suicide. The second is the *altruistic suicide*, caused by excessive integration that overwhelms the self. Any martyr is an altruistic suicide—Jesus Christ, according to First Peter, died for *our* sins. The third category, the *anomic suicide*, is a response to "critical [...] disturbances in the collective order" (267). The stockbroker who kills himself after Black Tuesday is an anomic suicide; so are the suicides in the wake of an apocalyptic event, like the woman who turns on the gas after the mass blindness that opens John Wyndham's *The Day of the Triffids* (1951). However, Durkheim argues that any upset, positive or negative, will have this effect. The suddenly rich are as vulnerable as the suddenly poor, since neither are prepared to navigate their new and foreign circumstances. He famously relegates his final category, the *fatalistic suicide*, to a single footnote. The fatalistic suicide occurs under "the inescapable and inflexible character of the rule over which one has no power" (305). Many suicides of slaves are fatalistic, as is the death pact between Oroonoko and Imoinda. Christie Davies and Mark Neal note that there is a symmetry to these categories: egotistical and anomic suicides are detached from society, the first through a lack of integration, the second through a lack of regulation, while altruistic and fatalistic suicides have an unhealthy attachment to society: an altruistic suicide is too integrated, a fatalistic suicide too regulated.[10] The elegance of this solution is no small part of its appeal.

To reach his conclusions, Durkheim challenges both the significance of nonsocial causes and the existence of free will. He denies a connection between suicide and "extra-social factors": these are race, "cosmic factors," meaning environmental influences such as temperature or time of day, suicide by imitation (now called suicide contagion), and "psychopathic states," like nervous disorders or alcoholism. This distinguishes Durkheim from his predecessors. Morselli, Westcott, and Strahan all entertained arguments about racial, geographical, and psychological causes. In *The Rules of the Sociological Method* (1895; translated into English 1939), Durkheim argues that "there are ways of acting, thinking and feeling which possess the remarkable property of existing outside the consciousness of the individual," a phenomenon he would later term the *conscience collective*.[11] He might be paraphrasing Morselli and his "really wonderful regularity of social phenomena" when he writes about "the outstanding regularity" with which these "recur in similar circumstances" (81). For Durkheim, what he calls *social facts* have a monopoly on causality. The *conscience collective* does not reflect or

[10] Christie Davies and Mark Neal, "Durkheim's Altruistic and Fatalistic Suicide," in *Durkheim's Suicide: A Century of Research and Debate*, ed. W. S. F. Pickering and Geoffrey Walford (Routledge, 2000), 37.

[11] Émile Durkheim, *The Rules of the Sociological Method and Selected Texts on Sociology and Its Method*, trans. W. D. Halls (Free Press, 2013), 20. All subsequent references are noted parenthetically in the text.

influence the actions of the individual—it determines them. We are only under the "illusion" that "we have ourselves produced what has been imposed on us externally" (22). This means the statistical accumulation of social facts renders the will of the individual irrelevant: "Since each one of these statistics includes without distinction all individual cases, the individual circumstances which may have played some part in producing the phenomenon cancel each other out and consequently do not contribute to determining the nature of the phenomenon" (24). He eliminates the individual from his equation like he is simplifying fractions. To each suicide he allows a "personal imprint," but their "movements" are "in reality the outcome and extension of a social state to which they give external form" (*Suicide* 306 and 331).

Were it not for his totalizing rhetoric—what Steven Lukes calls his "doctrinal instance on single-level explanation"—this would not be as much of a problem.[12] Still, Durkheim betrays an uneasiness around the complexities of psychology and its implications for the causes of behavior. Ruling out the need to examine individual cases, he explains, "This is because to attempt an inventory of all the characteristics peculiar to an individual is an insoluble problem. Every individual is an infinity, and infinity cannot be exhausted" (*Rules* 71). The grounds for exclusion are not that such an inventory would be useless; rather, that he cannot produce one. When he writes that consciousness gives us "muddled impressions" of the facts of individual psychology, that it "provides no clear, distinct notions or explanatory concepts," he is not disqualifying its value but complaining about the limits of scientific discourse in producing theories of subjective experience (*Rules* 8). On the question of observation, Durkheim admits defeat: "given the way in which most suicides are carried out, the observations that we would need to have are more or less impossible to obtain" (*Suicide* 148). On the question of intention, he determines it is "too subjective to be dealt with scientifically," then rules out its existence altogether, then takes his peers to task for relying on it in their explanations of behavior (*Rules* 82). With a suicide, he asks:

> How can one know what motive impelled the agent and whether, once he was resolved, it was death itself that he desired or some other outcome? Intention is too intimate a matter for it to be accessible from outside except by means of vague approximation. It even escapes internal observation. How often do we not ourselves mistake the true motives for our own acts!
>
> (*Suicide* 17–18)

[12] Steven Lukes, Introduction to *The Rules of the Sociological Method and Selected Texts on Sociology and Its Method* by Émile Durkheim (Free Press, 2013), 28.

Once again, the problem is not its relevance to the question but its elusive nature: too subjective, too intimate, inaccessible from the outside and even, sometimes, from within. Durkheim banishes psychological causes from sociology because they cannot be contained by the language of his discipline. Under these conditions, it is difficult to accept his claim that "the intrinsic nature of the acts that produce the outcome matters very little" (*Suicide* 16). Note the sterile euphemism "outcome" [*résultat*].[13]

Durkheim attempts to evade questions of motives and intention by substituting them with one about knowledge. His definition of suicide reads, "*Any case of death resulting directly or indirectly from a positive or negative act, carried out by the victim himself, which he was aware would produce this result*" (*Suicide* 19; emphasis in original). To classify a death as a suicide, the victim must have known they would die. There are clear problems with this distinction. For example, as Whitney Pope notes, knowledge is no less subjective than motive.[14] John Varty points out that the questions are related: without considering intention, how else could one determine whether the victim knew their actions would produce their death?[15] Moreover, Durkheim relies on official suicide statistics that must incorporate decisions about intention, about whether the victims did desire death. Officials did not rule a death a suicide unless they had positive evidence to suggest as much—that is, evidence of intention. Whether a suicide was aware that he or she would die was not the criterion. Durkheim argues that even if he did have access to the thoughts of the victims, the "reasons given for suicide or those that the suicide himself gives to explain his actions are, most often, only the apparent causes" (*Suicide* 154). Nevertheless, his data are based on these apparent causes. He insists that sociology should not be adulterated with psychology, but he cannot arrive at any meaningful conclusions without it. In essence, he is building a science of subjectivity disguised as objective discourse.

Certainly, Durkheim is right to argue that "the whole does not equal the sum of its parts," that society includes individuals while possessing characteristics that are unique to groups, but his refusal to supplement his arguments with nonsocial causes constitutes a significant explanatory failure (*Rules* 86). In his worldview, the whole determines the parts. Individuals do not create but are created by society. Emotions are not "generated" [*faits*] but "undergone" [*subis*]

[13] Émile Durkheim, *Le Suicide* (Ancienne Librairie Germer Baillière, 1897), 3.

[14] Pope, *Durkheim's Suicide: A Classic Analyzed*, 10–11.

[15] John Varty, "Suicide, Statistics, and Sociology: Assessing Douglas' Critique of Durkheim," in *Durkheim's Suicide: A Century of Research and Debate*, ed. W. S. F. Pickering and Geoffrey Walford (Routledge, 2000), 58–9.

(*Rules* 22).[16] This reversal of causality denies subjective experience its meaning—and its evidentiary value. His claim that "it is no longer acceptable to believe that a social fact is merely an individual fact generalized" leaves unwritten that he, in turn, views individual facts as merely social facts particularized (*Suicide* 143). The dehumanizing effects of his rhetoric are so prominent that Pope, during a discussion of Durkheimian integration, has to remind his readers that it "is people, of course, who are integrated."[17] The authoritarian stance precludes him from permitting the two approaches to complement rather than invalidate one another. Pope clarifies that "Durkheim investigated not suicide per se but social suicide rates," and this means he was unable "to explain who among the many possible candidates in a given social environment will actually commit suicide" (11 and 200). Richard Sennett, in an otherwise-laudatory introduction to *Suicide*, admits that "the text seems—at least to me—not to come to grips with the sentence, 'I want to die.'"[18] But suicide rates depend on who among the many possible candidates do commit suicide. If Durkheim cannot tell us why one and not another, if he cannot come to grips with the sentence, "I want to die," then he cannot exhaust the subject of voluntary death.

Detecting Suicide

The English detective is an expert. In contrast to the gumshoes of American noir, writes Ronald R. Thomas, the English "established the authority of a class of experts that could read someone's body like a text with the precision of a machine."[19] Where emotions often compromise the schemes of villains, the cold and precise detective is unclouded by human frailties, able to collect evidence and produce an almost mathematical answer to every puzzle they meet. Inspector Mallett is one such expert—he is on the scent by page sixteen. All the same, in the case of a suicide, machines are unnecessary. No authoritative reading is required. The body of Leonard Dickinson is legible to all. The claim that he "just wasn't that sort of person" is a common refrain in detective fiction, used to eliminate the possibility of suicide and rarely undermined by the resolution of the case. The specter of the suicidal type—the sort of person who *does* kill themselves—haunts

16 Émile Durkheim, *Les Règles de la Méthode Sociologique* (Librairie Félix Alcan, 1919), 10.

17 Pope, *Durkheim's Suicide: A Classic Analyzed*, 17.

18 Richard Sennett, Introduction to *On Suicide* by Émile Durkheim (Penguin, 2006), xvi.

19 Ronald R. Thomas, *Detective Fiction and the Rise of Forensic Science* (Cambridge University Press, 2003), 5.

both professional and amateur readings of suicidal bodies, and it enables most characters to make immediate and accurate determinations about whether a given corpse chose death.

Consider Christie's *Sparkling Cyanide* (1945), which opens with an apparent suicide: on her birthday, Rosemary Barton consumes the title drink, a glass of poisoned champagne. Her husband, George Barton—who is not the killer—knows she did not kill herself: "Rosemary was not at all a suicidal type."[20] She "loved life." Furthermore, "If by any chance Rosemary *had* contemplated doing away with herself, surely she'd never do it that way? Painful and—and ugly. An overdose of some sleeping stuff would be far more likely" (98; emphasis in original). Colonel Johnnie Race agrees: "He had thought her a singularly lovely nit-wit—but certainly not a melancholic type" (97). The murderer, as it happens, is Rosemary's cousin, Victor, who dangles the threat of suicide to pressure his mother, Lucille, into sending him money. Lucille worries he will shoot himself. Not George: "These people who threaten suicide never do it" (19). He is right about Victor, and he is right about Rosemary. Neither is the type—for suicide, at least.

Christie's "Dead Man's Mirror" (1937) ends its second chapter with a tease: "There was no need of speculation. The picture was clear. Sir Gervase Chevenix-Gore had shot himself" (127). Near the corpse, the word SORRY is printed on his blotting-pad. The answer is so obvious it must be wrong. After all, there are ten chapters left. Only Sir Gervase's wife, the spiritualist Lady Chevenix-Gore, falls for the ruse, frustrating Poirot's questions with unscientific talk of Fate, and Karma, and a Curse. The others are consistent. His son-in-law and land agent: "I simply can't imagine his thinking the world would be able to get on without him" (138). His lawyer and friend: "He should never have considered Sir Gervase the kind of man who would take his own life" (150). His adopted daughter: "It wasn't a bit like him" (176). Even his butler: "I never dreamed of such a thing" (144). Poirot, of course, doubts the scene "from the first" (189). Sir Gervase thought of himself as a Colossus. "Does such a man destroy himself?" he asks, answering his question like a catechism, "Surely not [...] *It is wrong psychologically*" (148; emphasis in original). Christie agrees, and the resolution involves a revised will, a secret marriage, and a disguised, avenging mother. It requires a Poirot to tell this story, but the staged suicide is legible to every witness, including the reader.

[20] Agatha Christie, *Sparkling Cyanide* (HarperCollins, 1992), 97. All subsequent references are noted parenthetically in the text.

These characters rely on nonsocial causes to justify the exclusion of suicide. They make no explicit appeal to religion, marital status, or nationality. Instead, it is *wrong psychologically*. Still, the psychological factors are definitive. They have the clarity and consistency of sociological conclusions. These are not clues, they are laws. Instead of introducing idiosyncratic details that would complicate the mystery and open it to a wider range of explanations, *wrong psychologically* closes an avenue of inquiry by assigning the victim a type. "Man is an unoriginal animal," Poirot says in *Cards on the Table* (1936). "No one can do a thing that is not *dans son caractère*!"[21] In a sense, Lady Chevenix-Gore is correct: Fate or a Curse, in the form of an immutable psychological profile, has determined the facts of the case. Hare's quotation from Thomas Browne does not in fact apply: Sir Gervase and Rosemary Barton are in the power of calamity, and Death is not their own.

Christie writes three suicides into *And Then There Were None* (1939), though one is dead before the novel begins. The other two, Vera and Wargrave, adhere to fairly conventional, if Victorian, comeuppance for a killer, much like Jackie in *Death on the Nile* (1937) (egotistical suicides, according to Durkheim). But several of the murders are ambiguous, beginning with the first, Marston's. Dr. Armstrong suggests prussic acid as the cause of death, probably potassium cyanide. Vera is suspicious: "You'd never think that *he* would kill himself. He was so alive. He was—oh—enjoying himself!" Blore concurs: "I shouldn't have said Mr. Marston was a suicidal type of gentleman."[22] Armstrong shares their doubts, and later, frustrated with the available evidence, he says, "Hang it all, I'm a doctor. I know something about suicides. Anthony Marston wasn't a suicidal type" (85). All three are correct, two without the expertise of being a physician. Type, understood to encompass both its older meaning as "that by which something is symbolized or figured" and its newer one as "the general form, structure, or character distinguishing a particular kind, group, or class of beings or objects," assesses the suicidal body based on clues gleaned through a combination of character, heritage, and social status (*OED*). Type demands that character and behavior are consistent across time, and for that reason, the surface clues of type are legible to every perceptive witness. Type is the currency of sociology. It is exhaustible, and here it is destiny. When it comes to suicide, the

21 Agatha Christie, *Cards on the Table* (Dell, 1936), 66, 206.

22 Agatha Christie, *And then There Were None* (Pocket Books, 1976), 52. Emphasis in original. All subsequent references are noted parenthetically in the text.

red herring fools very few. At the end of the novel, Blore's own ambiguous death is examined by an inspector and an assistant commissioner sorting through the wreckage. The inspector says, "Men don't commit suicide that way—and what's more Blore wasn't that kind of man. *We* knew Blore" (163; emphasis in original). The word this time around is the synonymous *kind*, but the meaning is the same: there are categories of people, and Blore did not fall under the category "suicidal." Again, he is correct. The bodies of Marston, Blore, and Armstrong are accurately read as murders, not suicides. Absent an Hercule Poirot, neither the victims nor the police can solve the case. They never identify the killer. However—excepting the murderer himself, who stages his suicide as another murder—professional and amateur alike can read the bodies of the authentic and inauthentic suicide. They know the type.

Dorothy L. Sayers solves the problem of the suicidal body by disposing of it for most of the novel. Since it is easy to read, it needs to go missing. In *Have His Carcase* (1932), the detective novelist Harriet Vane is on a beach near Wilvercombe when she finds the corpse of a gigolo, Paul Alexis Goldschmidt. He appears to have cut his throat, but he is wearing gloves, an odd choice under the circumstances. The death draws her friend, Sir Peter Wimsey, who concurs with her reading: "Why should anybody cut his throat in gloves?" (47). Unfortunately, the tide takes the body, and their suspicions cannot be confirmed for several hundred pages. Once again, the chorus mostly sings in tune. Here is Alexis' lover, Mrs. Weldon: "I *know*, I know absolutely, that poor Paul couldn't have—done anything rash" (62; emphasis in original). His colleague, Charis: "The minute I heard about it, I said to myself, 'That's not like Alexis.' He hadn't the nerve to do a thing like that. Why, he was terrified of pricking his little finger" (82). Another colleague, Doris: "And he'd have taken some sleeping-stuff [...] I know that, because he showed it to me once, when he was in one of his blue fits. 'That is my way out of the bad world,' he said, and he talked a lot of poetry" (83). And a third, Monsieur Antoine: "I cannot understand this business of throat-cutting. It is not reasonable. Why did Alexis go all that distance away? [...] If he had decided to suicide himself, he would have done it at home" (83). He is not the type, he is not the type to do it like *that*. Harriet agrees: Alexis had been led to believe he was about to inherit the Russian throne, and "young emperors on the point of leading successful revolutions do not commit suicide" (394). This is character analysis by way of axiom. Even without the evidence of the body to confirm their suspicions, they are all of them correct. Alexis was murdered. Only the coroner gets it wrong. He rules the death a suicide despite the lack of hesitation wounds, and he attributes the decision to the victim's excitable, Russian nature. He misreads the most important clue, the body itself, but he is not wrong for relying on type. He is wrong for misidentifying it. The reader, wiser than the expert, knows from the start that Alexis did not kill himself.

With the rare case of genuine suicide, the correct answer is the obvious answer: appearance reflects reality. In Christie's "Murder in the Mews" (1936), Inspector James Japp, the Scotland Yard man, outlines the chief points of the case to Poirot: Barbara Allen, engaged to a young Member of Parliament, was found dead with a Webley .25 in her right hand, the noise of the shot masked by celebrations of Guy Fawkes Day. "It looked a clear case of suicide," he tells the detective.[23] And yet, there is no note. The blotter is "an innocent white" (13). Poirot finds other inconsistencies and deduces that a friend, Jane Plenderleith, found the body, removed the note, and staged the scene as a murder to frame the man responsible for Mrs. Allen's suicide, her blackmailer. Miss Plenderleith, who knows better, relies on the same tropes that enable the casts of the above stories to discount voluntary death. She insists to Japp, "There was nothing in the world to make her commit suicide," and further, "Even if Barbara *did* kill herself, I can't imagine her *killing herself that way*" (20 and 22; emphasis in original). When pressed, she tops off her fiction with an anecdote: "we were discussing suicide once and she said much the easiest way would be to turn the gas on and stuff up all the cracks and just go to bed [...] I said I'd far rather shoot myself. And she said no, she could never shoot herself" (22). She sounds like every honest witness quoted above.

It looks like a clear case of suicide, and despite some tampering, it is. How often is Scotland Yard right *before* Poirot arrives? After all, part of the fun is watching the police insist on a theory that is clearly false to both detective and reader. The detective is trained to treat each clue, each piece of evidence with suspicion. The character is the dramatic embodiment of the hermeneutics of skepticism: "The critic, like the detective, refuses to take surface meanings at face value; the text, like the criminal suspect, must be scrutinized, interrogated, and made to yield its hidden secrets," writes Rita Felski. "Interpretation pivots on a skeptical and adversarial relationship to its object [...] ordinary readers, just like the hapless Watson, are easily deceived by the evidence of their eyes."[24] With

[23] Agatha Christie, *Murder in the Mews and Three Other Poirot Cases* (Fontana, 1989), 10. All subsequent references are noted parenthetically in the text.

[24] Rita Felski, "Suspicious Minds," *Poetics Today* 32, no. 2 (Summer 2011), 224.

cases of murders staged like suicides, this adversarial skepticism is vindicated, even if little of it is required. With "Murder in the Mews," the evidence of your eyes does not deceive. What you see is what you get, and the authority of Thomas's class of experts only works to obscure the answer to the puzzle. Since Miss Plenderleith is aware of her audience, she plots her scheme according to their biases. When Poirot has finally solved the case, he shares his "picture" of the crime. This includes "a note" and is, he fancies, "a very moving letter [...] A young, gentle, unhappy woman driven by blackmail to take her life" (60). He is not half wrong, and Miss Plenderleith brings the picture into focus: "She said she loved Charles and couldn't live without him, but that for his own sake she mustn't marry him. She was taking the best way out, she said" (61). Strahan would call this a quasi-suicide, Durkheim an altruistic one. It is calm, measured, and rational. She assesses her situation, determines that voluntary death is the best solution, and acts accordingly. This is the kind of suicide detective fiction can accommodate.

The sociological turn in the study of suicide shifted the emphasis to its causes, which Durkheim and his contemporaries insist are social causes. The effects, the treatment of the suicide as a crime or a sin, are irrelevant. Durkheim is documenting behavior; he is not defining its meaning in moral terms. Depictions of voluntary death in Golden Age detective fiction, which tends to view human behavior as a calculable series of variables, illustrate both the influence and the limitations of the sociological approach. Consider, in contrast Leonard Dickinson or Paul Alexis Goldschmidt, the historical example of Cato the Younger. According to Plutarch, when his enemy approached Utica, Cato called for his sword. His servants, fearing self-murder, disobeyed him, and he "smote one on the mouth with his fist."[25] He gave his hand to a physician, and "this made everybody more cheerful, since they thought he had a mind to live" (130). Cato then fell on his sword. The physician was able "replace his bowels, which remained uninjured, and to sew up the wound" (131). Cato then "pushed the physician away, tore his bowels with his hands, rent the wound still more, and so died." The bandages are a red herring, a signal to the witnesses that Cato is safe, as no rational person would attend to minor wounds if he intended to kill himself. The gruesome and protracted suicide that follows belies such a reading. The miscommunication lies in a false sense of shared values: Cato does

[25] Plutarch, "Parallel Lives," in *The Ethics of Suicide: Historical Sources*, ed. Margaret Pabst Battin (Oxford University Press, 2015), 129. All subsequent references are noted parenthetically in the text.

not abide by the same rules as men who believe that life should be preserved at all costs. My point here is not that these signals are never trustworthy but that they are unreliable. Suicide is too diverse a practice for such consistencies. Ambiguous and multicausal, it is difficult to capture through scientific methods alone. The available evidence fails to furnish a complete answer. This is an image of suicide that is incompatible with detective fiction or with the forensic science and sociology to which it owes its vision of human nature. It is a suicide that does not adhere to reason, that is illegible to its witnesses, and that resists categorization. It is a case Poirot could not have solved, perhaps because solving relies on a model of investigation that cannot abide irresolution, a model that excludes, because it cannot see, those who choose death. Sometimes, a suicide does leave out an apple for the following morning.

6

The Gospel of the Death Drive: Blood Knowledge and Suicide in D. H. Lawrence's *Women in Love*

Despite a keen interest in psychoanalysis, there is no evidence that D. H. Lawrence read Sigmund Freud.[1] In fact, despite friendships with several of its practitioners, he is only definitively known to have read one book on the subject, Carl Jung's *Psychology of the Unconscious* (1912).[2] Nevertheless, with characteristic Lawrencian brazenness, he went ahead and wrote a veritable dissertation on psychoanalysis, a new psychology of sorts, and the result was a pair of monographs, *Psychoanalysis and the Unconscious* (1921) and *Fantasia of the Unconscious* (1922). In these books, Lawrence rejects the neurotic basis of Freud's diagnoses, but he does reiterate much of Freud's arguments. This includes what is in effect a variation of the death drive, one that both echoes and diverges from Jung, Freud, and their common source, Sabina Spielrein's "Destruction as the Cause of Coming into Being" (1912; translated into English 1994). In *Psychoanalysis* and *Fantasia*, Lawrence advocates for what he calls "blood knowledge" over "mental knowledge," for instinct over intellect, arguing that destruction, conflict, and rupture are the necessary conditions of both personal and cultural rebirth. Of course, this idea was not exclusive to psychoanalysis. The fluidity between life and death and the conception of time as cyclical rather than linear permeated the culture and, in particular, Lawrence's reading of James George Frazer and Helena Blavatsky.[3] But as contemporaries

[1] Bruce Steele, "Introduction" to *Psychoanalysis and the Unconscious and Fantasia of the Unconscious* by D. H. Lawrence (Cambridge University Press, 2014), 28.

[2] Steele, Introduction to *Psychoanalysis and the Unconscious and Fantasia of the Unconscious*, 29.

[3] D. H. Lawrence, *The Letters of D.H. Lawrence Volume II: June 1913—October 1916*, ed. George J. Zytaruk and James T. Boulton (Cambridge University Press, 1981), 470 and D. H. Lawrence, *The Letters of D.H. Lawrence Volume III: October 1916—June 1921*, ed. James T. Boulton and Andrew Robertson (Cambridge University Press, 1984), 150. All subsequent references are noted parenthetically in the text.

who came to similar conclusions about the facts but antithetical conclusions about their meaning, Freud and Lawrence serve as useful foils to one another.

In the following chapter, I will argue that blood knowledge is the force that motivates Gerald Crich's suicide in *Women in Love* (1920). Read in these terms, both the devastation of the First World War and the suicide of Gerald represent not the endpoint of civilization but the possibility of its restoration—what Andrew Harrison calls "the embrace of war as a means to clearing away the old and ushering in the new."[4] This constitutes a significant departure from critical consensus, which views Gerald's death as a failure. David J. Gordon is typical in his position that he is "damned because he will not see and follow the true path to salvation,"[5] while Harrison, who incorporates creative destruction into his analysis, nonetheless argues that in *Women in Love*, the "process of coming through violence to new forms of life" is "subordinated to a sense of tragic fate and wasteful destructiveness," represented by characters who are "stillborn, frozen, [and] wounded."[6] In contrast, I argue that Lawrence uses Gerald to champion his version of the death drive, enacting and celebrating the kind of regression that Freud only describes. This is not wasteful but creative destruction. Because Lawrence understands suicide in mythological rather than psychological terms, Gerald's death is a microcosm, a gesture, an individualized manifestation of the civilizational death drive that presages cultural resurrection. It is akin to the ancient Roman practice of anthropomancy, or divination by entrails.

Lawrence and Psychoanalysis

Lawrence appreciated *Psychology and the Unconscious* enough to send it along to Katherine Mansfield (*III* 301–2). With his mythological inclinations, his rejection of the Oedipus complex, and his own Oedipal break from a man he once addressed as "the father," Jung held obvious appeal for Lawrence.[7] In *Psychology of the Unconscious*, Jung redefines the libido as "all the unknown and countless manifestations of the Will in the sense of Schopenhauer," which would have satisfied Lawrence's frustration with the psychoanalytic reduction of

4 Andrew Harrison, *D.H. Lawrence and Italian Futurism: A Study of Influence* (Rodopi, 2003), 111.
5 David J. Gordon, "D.H. Lawrence's Dual Myth of Origin," *The Sewanee Review* 89, no. 1 (Winter 1981), 86.
6 Harrison, *D.H. Lawrence and Italian Futurism*, 132.
7 Peter Gay, *Freud: A Life for Our Time* (Norton, 1998), 227.

all interactions to sex.[8] Indeed, his own definition of sex as "the fountain head, where life bubbles up into the person from the unknown" hews much closer to Jung's Will than Freud's libido (*II* 102). Most important for our purposes, it was through Jung that Lawrence was exposed to Spielrein's concept of destruction as the necessary condition of creation, which Freud would develop into the death drive. Naturally, the point of entry for Jung is mythological. At the river Styx, death and life are conflated, and man wishes "that the black water of death might be the water of life; that death, with its cold embrace, might be the mother's womb" (245). In Christian legend, the crucifix is transformed into the tree of life, and in "psychologic thought [...] death is interpreted as entrance into the mother's womb" (269). For the adolescent, the arrival of sexuality augurs the death of childhood, and ultimately, "the highest summit of life is expressed through the symbolism of death [...] for creation beyond one's self means personal death," as the "coming generation is the end of the preceding one" (320). Jung argues for a cyclical model of nature which positions death as the beginning of new life, a necessary condition for rebirth. He also reiterates Spielrein's suggestion that creation, or procreation, is essentially suicidal in demanding the "personal death" of the creator.[9]

Lawrence had been toying with similar ideas before he read Jung in December 1918 (*III* 301). In the *Study of Thomas Hardy* (1914), two years after Spielrein published "Destruction"—but long before it was translated into English—Lawrence attributes progress to a drive toward self-expression and stasis to a drive toward self-preservation. Like Spielrein, he associates self-preservation with stagnation and death, self-expression with death and rebirth. In our current condition, we are "sealed in our own self-preservation as dying chrysalides," dying because we remain chrysalides, because we choose the self-preserving safety of the cocoon over the self-expressive rebirth outside the cocoon.[10] Rather than the machine life of modernity, Lawrence advocates for "real, utter satisfaction," which requires the subject to give themselves over "to complete quivering uncertainty, to sentient non-knowledge" (35). He will later term this "blood knowledge," an embrace of the primitive over the civilized, a religion of

[8] C. G. Jung, *Psychology of the Unconscious*, trans. Beatrice M. Hinkle (Dover, 2002), 135–6. All subsequent references are noted parenthetically in the text.

[9] Quoting Jung, she writes, "Our descendants become our most dangerous enemies for whom we are unprepared. They will survive and take power from our enfeebled hands." Sabina Spielrein, "Destruction as the Cause of Coming into Being," trans. Kenneth McCormick, *Journal of Analytical Psychology* 39, no. 2 (1994), 155. All subsequent references are noted parenthetically in the text.

[10] D. H. Lawrence, *Study of Thomas Hardy and Other Essays*, ed. Bruce Steele (Cambridge University Press, 2002), 16. All subsequent references are noted parenthetically in the text.

sensation instead of intellect. For Lawrence, suicide is one means of achieving blood knowledge: "let us tip-cat with death," he writes of the war, "let us rush throwing our lives away" (16). Then, "at any rate we shall have a sensation—and 'perhaps,' after all, the value of life is in death." Tip-cat is a baseball-like game, so Lawrence is evoking an image of bodies being lobbed one after another into the trenches. His contemporaries, of course, would read this as a tragedy—as would he in other contexts—but *Thomas Hardy* suggests that the mass suicide of the First World War may in fact be a form of destructive creation, a sort of communal shock that jump-starts our relationship with blood knowledge. We must lose our lives to save them; we must die to be reborn. One implication of such a theology is that suicide, robbed of its finality, becomes a generative act. Resurrection is born in the ashes of our combustion.

Seven years later, after reading *Psychology of the Unconscious*, Lawrence begins *Fantasia* with the argument that the process of individuation requires a rent or rupture, "the individual asserting himself beyond all ties or claims."[11] This assertion, in its destruction of a shared consciousness for the purpose of creating a separate subject, mutilates both parent and child. In a broader context, it takes on larger significance: when a tree puts forth

> new green tips [...] each new tip arises out of the apparent death of the old, the preceding one. Old leaves have got to fall, old forms must die [...] And dead leaves make good mold. And so do dead men.
>
> (189)[12]

For Lawrence, modern man is singing his swan song, but instead of a healthy self-destruction, he is condemned to perish by "this ghastly white disease of self-conscious idealism"—that is, mental knowledge (118). This disease has arrested the civilizational cycle of destruction and rebirth, and the solution for Lawrence is in rejecting self-consciousness for "that other reality, our own true spontaneous self." The connection to suicide is now explicit: "men with any backbone would rather kill themselves than go on with it—or kill somebody else." This choice will be borne out in *Women in Love*, which has Gerald attempting to murder Gudrun before committing suicide, but for the purpose of intergenerational evolution,

[11] D. H. Lawrence, *Psychoanalysis and the Unconscious and Fantasia of the Unconscious*, ed. Bruce Steele (Cambridge University Press, 2014), 77. All subsequent references are noted parenthetically in the text.

[12] At his most fanciful, Lawrence writes that death was the condition required for the creation of the cosmos: "out of the death of living creatures, when their little living bodies fell dead and fell asunder into all sorts of matter and forces and energies, sun, moons, stars and worlds," punctuating with wry concision, "So you got the universe" (70).

blood knowledge demands mass destruction. According to this logic, the "war was really not a bad beginning," if not for the fact that it was fought "under the banners of idealism," and moreover that it ended, forcing the British home again to "the virus [...] rotting their very souls." Along with his curt dismissal of the war dead ("And so do dead man"), the casual tone here emphasizes that a Lawrencian vision of history, and of suicide, is bereft of any affective and phenomenological concerns. He is comfortable with mass violence so long as it triggers a return to man's primitive focus on physicality and spontaneity over hesitant intellectualism.

This constitutes a crucial difference between Lawrence's death drive and that of Freud. For Freud, the death drive was a symptom produced by the disease of life—it was never the cure. Lawrence, on the other hand, would make mulch of the charnel. He, like Spielrein, Freud, and Jung, sees destruction as the cause of creation, but his focus and concern are with the creative outcome, not the destructive condition of that outcome. Bruce Steele writes that one of Lawrence's primary quarrels with the discipline rested in its "view of the human person derived from illness and disorder, not from health or wholeness as he believed it should," and the same is true of their positions on death and self-destruction.[13] The difference is not substantial but perspectival. What Freud saw as illness, Lawrence saw as health. Where Freud saw modern neurosis, Lawrence saw something like an ancient, primitivist, and cyclical rite of history, one that offered humanity potential salvation. For Lawrence, the neurosis was choosing life and mental knowledge over blood knowledge and death.

Lawrence's Fictional Suicides

While Lawrence began his fictional explorations of the subject as early as *The Trespasser* (1912), the suicide in that novel is less twentieth-century death drive and more eighteenth-century *Sturm und Drang*. When Siegmund hangs himself with the straps of his portmanteau, it is what Holly A. Laird calls suicide "as conventional tragic show stopper."[14] A few years later and only months into the First World War, Lawrence wrote "Eloi, Eloi, Lama Sabachthani?" (1915). The energetic, repetitive, and overflowing prosody recalls Walt Whitman, the

13 Steele, Introduction, 30.

14 Holly A. Laird, "Suicide in D.H. Lawrence's *Women in Love*: A Modernist Ethics," in *New D.H. Lawrence*, ed. Howard J. Booth (Manchester University Press, 2009), 60.

poem a kind of deathly "Song of Myself" (1855). The speaker begins, "How I hate myself, this body which is me," lamenting that self-destruction remains prohibited by law, "for it is written against me I must not, / I must preserve my life from hurt" (1 and 5–6).[15] Still, the war provides him with solace, as it is a mass self-destruction that acts as relief in the wake of his own frustrated suicide: "how glad I am to hear the shells / [...] That gives me peace" (9 and 15). For his own death, the speaker finds a circuitous route: "I kill my shadow's shadow of me!" (25). In other words, he heads to the trenches, where he finds his double in a German soldier. Rather than killing himself, he kills the German, but since he sees no difference between brother and enemy, between self and other, the murder is a sublimated suicide. His shadow's shadow is, of course, himself. Lawrence has therefore reversed Freud's early formula in "Mourning and Melancholia" (1917; translated into English 1925). Instead of explaining suicide as the murderous impulse directed inward, he sees murder as the suicidal impulse directed outward. The ethos of blood knowledge is clear: better to kill oneself rather than remain shackled to a body that is "agony" (18). However, since the law—the fruits of mental knowledge—prohibits suicide, the trenches are the speaker's best recourse.

The murder is also a sexual act. Penis and bayonet are figured interchangeably, their meanings as generative and destructive objects likewise conflated:

> Like a bride he took my bayonet, wanting it,
> Like a virgin the blade of my bayonet, wanting it,
> And it sank to rest from me in him,
> And I, the lover, am consummate,
> And he is the bride, I have sown him with the seed
> And planted and fertilised him.
>
> (37–42)

The encounter reads like a rape, notwithstanding—or perhaps because of—the speaker's refrain-like insistence on his virgin bride "wanting it." For Lawrence, this type of assault provides the metaphorical confluence of destructive and creative impulses: it is a violence that can spawn a child, a murder as well as a fertilization. Finally, he asks, "What I beget, must I beget of blood? / Are the guns and the steel the bridegroom, / Our flesh the bride?" (52–4). The transformation from bridegroom to bride suggests that, in addition to his metaphorical suicide through the murder of the German, he will have an opportunity for a literal one

[15] D. H. Lawrence, *The Poems Volume III: Uncollected Poems and Early Versions*, ed. Christopher Pollnitz (Cambridge University Press, 2018). All subsequent references are to line numbers and noted parenthetically in the text.

in the arms of another soldier. On a psychological level, the war offers death to anyone who wants it. In the speaker's mind, his penetration of the German soldier is an assisted suicide. On a global scale, this accumulation of suicides is precisely the kind of mass self-destruction necessary for spiritual rebirth. The title, "Eloi, Eloi, Lama Sabachthani," is a reference to Christ, which suggests martyrdom, or suicide for the purpose of resurrection. Indeed, Christ was one of Spielrein's examples of the death drive. In his letters, Lawrence likewise posed as a Christ figure, the war his crucifixion (166). Four months before the publication of the poem, he wrote to Lady Cynthia Asquith:

> The [declaration of] War finished me: it was the spear through the side of all sorrows and hopes [...] All the while, I swear, my soul lay in the tomb—not dead, but with the flat stone over it, a corpse, become corpse cold [...] And all the time I knew I should have to rise again.
>
> (*II* 268–9)

Even in his blackest moods, Lawrence implies a sense of hope through the comparison to Christ: despite Longinus, despite burial, he will rise again. "Eloi, Eloi, Lama Sabachthani?" is closer to death; on the cross, Christ quotes Psalm 22:1, "My god, my god, why hast thou forsaken me?" (Mark 15:34). In the immediate aftermath of the Marne, of Tannenberg and the Masurian Lakes, "Eloi, Eloi" emphasizes doubt and despair; the poem ends with the speaker walking the "earth [...] Cleansed and in concord from the bed of death" (91 and 93).

By *Women in Love*, Lawrence's position was firmer and more optimistic. Nevertheless, Lawrence was unsettled by the novel. "The book frightens me: it is so end-of-the-world," he wrote to the novelist Catherine Carswell. "But it is, it must be, the beginning of a new world too" (*III* 25–6). This now-familiar cycle of devastation followed by rehabilitation—Birkin will call it "the flood of destructive creation"—courses through *Women in Love*.[16] For example, when Birkin discusses the concept of blood knowledge with Ursula, he continually emphasizes self-destruction as its precondition:

> It is death to one self—but it is the coming into being of another [...] You've got to lapse out before you can know what sensual reality is, lapse into unknowingness, and give up your volition [...] You've got to learn not-to-be, before you can come into being.
>
> (43–4)

[16] D. H. Lawrence, *Women in Love*, ed. David Farmer, Lindeth Vasey, and John Worthen (Cambridge University Press, 1987), 172. All subsequent references are noted parenthetically in the text.

This, of course, is an elephantine allusion to literary suicide, and by the end of the novel, Gerald will enact Birkin's "death to one self" and follow Hamlet into voluntary death. Meanwhile, Birkin will please Ursula with the "pleasant fancy" of an apocalypse, which he, like the speaker in "Eloi, Eloi," views as a cleansing: "If only man was swept off the face of the earth, creation would go on so marvellously, with a new start [...] think what lovely things would come out of the liberated days; things straight out of the fire" (128). Here Lawrence employs a phoenix-adjacent metaphor, as he did in *Thomas Hardy* when he asked, "Can I not be born again, save out of my own ashes, save in resurrection from the dead?" (80). By the time Birkin tells Gudrun, "If we are the end, we are not the beginning," she is fluent enough in his philosophy—and at this point, frankly, so are we—to reply, "The beginning comes out of the end" (173). Lawrence rehearses this form of transformation, of rebirth in the wake of death, over and over again in *Women in Love.*

Apocalypse, ashes, death—all are on full display in the opening pages of the novel. After only a few paragraphs, the Brangwen sisters find themselves "confronted by a void, a terrifying chasm" (10). Off the main road, "past a black patch of common-garden [...] sooty cabbage stumps stood shameless" (11). To Gudrun, their country is "an underworld," or an underworld carried to the surface, since "colliers bring it above-ground with them, shovel it up." The second image evokes trench warfare and its scarring of the French landscape, while the first reminds us that our common inheritance has been fouled by mechanization and modernity. Allied victory has arrested any spiritual progress the war made in providing an outlet for the embrace of blood knowledge and creative destruction. Cabbage *stumps,* denoting the "portion of the trunk of a felled tree," also suggest the word's primary definition as the "part remaining of an amputated or broken-off limb," an image commonly associated with Great War veterans (*OED*). Nature, like man, has emerged from Versailles disfigured, enervated.

For Gudrun, it is all a Platonic shadow: "Everything is a ghoulish replica of the real world," she tells Ursula, "a replica, a ghoul, all soiled, everything sordid." Even in "the purer country of the other side," that is, at the upper-class wedding the sisters watch from a distance, each of the attendees looks "like a character in a book, or a subject in a picture, or a marionette in a theatre, a finished creation" (12 and 14). The colliers, like the Tommies, have been reduced to a function in a machine—a consequence of Gerald's rationalism—but even the bright young things of Willey Green seem to follow a script. For Lawrence, who holds spontaneity as sacred, such automatism is the nadir of modernity. Gudrun's solution, at least, is simple: "She would have liked them all annihilated, cleared away, so that the world was left clear for her" (13). Her words can sound harsh or nihilistic to a reader unfamiliar with Lawrence's non-fiction, but in light of *Fantasia* and *Thomas Hardy*, this represents a shimmer of possibility—recall that the "war was really not a bad beginning." What Lawrence is writing is not glum mimesis, or baggy-eyed fatalism, but the first two panels in a triptych that ends with resurrection—Bosch's *The Garden of Earthly Delights* (*c.*1490–1510) in reverse. It is the middle panel, the in-between state, the process of transformation, that draws most of his attention.

What might the middle panel look like? Fortunately, Lawrence has provided us with both a mouthpiece, Rupert Birkin, and a case study, Gerald Crich, a veteran of "the last war" (64). Birkin's philosophy is helpfully outlined in a letter he writes to an indiscreet acquaintance, Halliday, who amuses himself by reading it aloud to friends in a much-cited example of Lawrence's ability to satirize his own proclamation-prone style.[17] Yet even in humor Lawrence plays the earnest prophet, and like a Trojan horse, the proclamation enters the narrative nonetheless, hidden inside his self-deprecation:

> There is a phase in every race [...] when the desire for destruction overcomes every other desire. In the individual, this desire is ultimately a desire for destruction in the self [...] It is a desire for the reduction-process in oneself, a reducing back to the origin [...] to the original rudimentary conditions of being ... And in the great retrogression, the reducing back of the created body of life, we get knowledge, and beyond knowledge, the phosphorescent ecstasy of acute sensation.
>
> (383)

Birkin links suicide to a larger, racial desire for destruction, one that yields blood knowledge, a knowledge that transcends mental knowledge, "the phosphorescent ecstasy of acute sensation." It is like Wordsworth's dictum arrested mid-sentence: Lawrence is looking simply for "the spontaneous overflow of powerful feelings," recollection and tranquility be damned. Returning to a pre-mental state, the subject becomes conscious on a level that privileges physicality over thought, sensation over reflection. For Lawrence, the suicide, the person who desires "destruction in the self," is a component or a microcosm of a larger restorative

[17] See, for example, Mark Kinkead-Weekes, "Violence in *Women in Love*," in *D.H. Lawrence's Women in Love: A Casebook*, ed. David Ellis (Oxford University Press, 2006), 240.

effort, "the reducing back of the created body of life" that leads to blood knowledge. The connection, perhaps, is inevitable. Could any human action serve Lawrence better as a metaphor for the mass destruction that was necessary to usher in a messianic resurrection than suicidal martyrdom?

Suicide as restoration: the argument is Lawrencian, but it is also Freudian. Despite his reading in Jung, and Jung's source in Spielrein, it is actually *Beyond the Pleasure Principle* (1920; translated into English 1922) that *Women in Love* most resembles. This short book was written after but published before Lawrence's novel, and its thesis is pressing enough to appear in italics: there is "*an urge inherent in organic life to restore an earlier state of things* which the living entity has been obliged to abandon under the pressure of external disturbing forces."[18] For Freud, it follows that this state must be actual rather than imaginative, a "state from which the living entity has at one time or other departed and to which it is striving to return" (45). There is only one such state or one possible endpoint to a series of regressions: therefore, again in italics, "*the aim of all life is death*" (46). Up to this point, Lawrence and Freud more or less agree. Both have identified a human urge toward self-destruction that manifests in both the individual and the culture at large. Freud, however, was not an advocate for suicide or for the indiscriminate killing of large numbers of people. He identified the death drive as a psychological and even a cultural phenomenon, but he didn't become a partisan for it. Even so, in *Civilization and Its Discontents* (1930; translated into English the same year), Freud does argue that civilization, an extension of our sexual instincts, "is largely responsible for our misery," admitting, "we should be much happier if we gave it up and returned to primitive conditions."[19] Such a return echoes the death drive, with its *earlier state of things*. Is the ultimate primitive condition death? Freud never answers the question his argument raises: if both civilization and modern sexuality cause neurotic misery, if a return to the primitive would bring us happiness, and if the aim of such a return is "the inanimate state," wouldn't that mean that self-destruction is preferable to reproduction (*Pleasure Principle* 46)? That life is the sickness, neuroses its symptoms, suicide its cure?

Lawrence, it appears, has both predicted the question and provided an answer: the complete destruction of civilization, a kind of a flood or deluge from which we can emerge reborn. He believed that the novel of the future would "take

[18] Sigmund Freud, *Beyond the Pleasure Principle*, trans. James Strachey (Norton, 1989), 43. All subsequent references are noted parenthetically in the text.

[19] Sigmund Freud, *Civilization and Its Discontents*, trans. James Strachey (Norton, 1989), 38.

the place of gospels," and *Women in Love* (which was at one point titled "The Latter Days" [*II* 659]) is his new testament, the gospel of the death drive.[20] In Freudian terms, this means Lawrence is *enacting* rather than just *chronicling* the drive: he is indulging the urge, all the while transcribing the experience as best he can. In Lawrencian terms, he is advocating for a large-scale transformation that transcends ethical objections to the deaths of men or to the suicide of an individual. He is relieving the pressure of life's external disturbing forces in order to begin a process of restoration to "the original rudimentary conditions of being," conditions whose value far exceeds their cost. Gerald, a veteran of the Boer War and accordingly familiar with an embrace of the death drive, whose project of industrialization initially aligns him with mental knowledge, continues the conversation that began in "Eloi, Eloi." Laird reads him as "an 'omen' of the greater social failure, a 'mastodon' that has failed to develop, a 'polar-bear' stranded at one pole"—in other words, as a dying chrysalid or a stillborn baby—but I would argue that it is the world of the novel as a whole that is failing to develop, rather than Gerald in particular.[21] He is not only the last of the mastodons but also the first of a new species, his suicide a gesture toward the apocalyptic and blood-soaked spiritual cleansing that Lawrence views as a requisite for evolution.

Early in the novel, Gerald examines the art in Halliday's rooms and sees something of a self-reflection:

> There were several negro statues, wood-carvings from West Africa, strange and disturbing, the carved negroes looked almost like the foetus of a human being. One was of a woman sitting naked in a strange posture, and looking tortured, her abdomen stuck out [...] she was sitting in childbirth, clutching the ends of the band that hung from her neck, one in each hand, so that she could bear down, and help labour. The strange, transfixed, rudimentary face of the woman again reminded Gerald of a foetus, it was also rather wonderful, conveying the extreme of physical sensation, beyond the limits of mental consciousness.
>
> (74)

The inspiration is assuredly primitivist, and the recognition of the self in the other is a trope that did not originate with Lawrence. It is, after all, the premise of Joseph Conrad's *Heart of Darkness* (1899). Still, Lawrence did spend much of his life searching for a reality that would match his imagined version

20 D. H. Lawrence, "The Future of the Novel," in *Study of Thomas Hardy and Other Essays*, ed. Bruce Steele (Cambridge University Press, 2002), 155.

21 Laird, "Suicide in D.H. Lawrence's *Women in Love*," 74.

of the primitive, ultimately finding disappointment in the real people he met in Australia, the United States, and Mexico. For Lawrence, ancient, non-European religions better understood blood knowledge than the spiritually emaciated Europeans of the twentieth century. Like Pablo Picasso in painting, he invents an image of West Africa, a region he never visited, to suit his artistic and polemical needs. Specifically, the statue's mixture of life and death forces—of childbirth and torture, of the shared prenatal development with the fetus and postpartum individuation of the mother—offers Gerald an image of creation through self-mutilation. The mother is herself a fetus, which further undermines the Whig narrative against which Lawrence is writing. History is not linear but cyclical, something suggested even in her posture, in the semicircular, crescent moon shape she assumes while bearing down for labor. Gerald is disgusted—"You can't call it *high* art"—but Birkin assures him it represents "pure culture in sensation, culture in the physical consciousness, really ultimate *physical* consciousness, mindless, utterly sensual. It is so sensual as to be final, supreme" (79; emphasis in original). Birkin is clearly enthusiastic, but he is also reminding us of the death that comes with blood knowledge, linking "*physical* consciousness" with words like *ultimate*, *final*, and *supreme*.

Later, during another of his lectures, Birkin says, "the West Africans, controlled by the burning death-abstraction of the Sahara, had been fulfilled in sun-destruction, the putrescent mystery of sun-rays," whereas the "white races, having the arctic north behind them, the vast abstraction of ice and snow, would fulfil a mystery of ice-destructive knowledge, snow-abstract annihilation" (254). Significantly, the West Africans have already fulfilled their divine purpose, while the "white races" are still awaiting their transformation.[22] Lawrence makes it patently clear whom he has nominated to represent them, and in the novel's conclusion, he will use Gerald's suicide in the Alps as an illustration of snow-abstract annihilation. To begin, consider the avalanche of metaphors Lawrence uses to introduce Gerald. In the opening scene of the novel, Gudrun recognizes "something northern" about him that "magnetised her," a pun on the arctic poles. His hair has "a glisten like cold sunshine refracted through crystals," his look is "new, unbroached, pure as an arctic thing" (14). She can't identify his age—perhaps he is thirty, perhaps older—and he kindles a feeling of "nostalgia" in her (15). This apparent contradiction—new and unbroached but timeless and

[22] "Us awful whites with our machines," Lawrence later wrote to Harriet Monroe and D. H. Lawrence, *The Letters of D.H. Lawrence Volume V: March 1924—March 1927*, ed. James T. Boulton and Lindeth Vasey (Cambridge University Press, 1989), 28.

an object of nostalgia—can only be reconciled if *new* and *old* are synonyms, as they would be under this cyclical model of history. Gerald is new because he embodies what is to come, and he is old because, according to Lawrence's prophecy, a revival of the old is precisely what is coming. Flip forward 200 pages and you find Birkin similarly rapt:

> He was one of these strange white wonderful demons from the north, fulfilled in the destructive frost mystery. And was he fated to pass away in this knowledge, this one process of frost-knowledge, death by perfect cold? Was he a messenger, an omen of the universal dissolution into whiteness and snow?
>
> (254)

The answer, considered in light of his ultimate death, is unmistakable. When Gerald and Gudrun finally consummate their relationship—the scene will encompass both of Lawrence's meanings of the word—he will remind her of "an apparition, the young Hermes" (343). An "apparition," of course, is a message from the afterworld, a life after death, and like that messenger of the gods, who traveled between the worlds of the mortal and the divine, Gerald bears at least one message himself: his suicide, a herald of the destruction that resurrection demands. In an unkind moment, Lawrence wrote that the poet Richard Barham Middleton "only really expressed himself once—when he killed himself" (*II* 102). Gerald's suicide is another such expression, another dramatic break from an otherwise-unremarkable life.

Back in Halliday's room, Gerald turns and notices "one or two new pictures in the room, in the Futurist manner," which along with "some ordinary London lodging-house furniture of the better sort, completed the whole" (74). F. T. Marinetti, who in his "Manifesto of Futurism" championed "the enthusiastic fervor of the primordial elements," declared war "the only hygiene of the world," glorified "the destructive gesture of anarchists," *and* fantasized about being murdered by his successors, shares much common intellectual ground with Lawrence—and with the Freud of *Totem and Taboo* (1913; translated into English 1918).[23] Lawrence did admire the Futurists' passionate rejection of tradition, and he certainly shared their love of hyperbole, but he ultimately found their solution, enthralled as it was by modernity, untenable. Lawrence wrote to Arthur McLeod, "They will progress down the purely male or intellectual or scientific purpose"—in other words, they are limited by mental knowledge or the "ultra-ultra

[23] F. T. Marinetti, "The Founding and Manifesto of Futurism," trans. Lawrence Rainey, in *Futurism: An Anthology*, ed. Christine Poggi Rainey and Laura Wittman (Yale University Press, 2009), 51.

intellectual" (*II* 181). To Garnett, he was blunter: "The futurists are stupid [...] they will only look for the phenomena of the science of physics to be found in human being" (ibid. 183). By grouping their paintings with furniture "of the better sort," as just another commodity for the bohemian collector, Lawrence dismisses their authenticity, their integrity, and therefore the truth value of their museum-razing message of creation through destruction.[24] He clearly favors the "strange and disturbing" statue, and in this scene, he stages the West African fulfillment of creative self-destruction confronting its northern counterpart. Gerald has yet to approach the mystery of ice-destructive knowledge, but by the end of the novel, as Charles L. Ross observes, he will be "frozen into a northern fetish statue."[25]

First, he must undergo a symbolic transformation in "Death and Love," a chapter with a title that syntactically couples the opposing forces of destruction and creation, ordering love as succeeding death and hinting at its generative potential. True to its name, "Death and Love" prepares the reader for Gerald's suicide by metaphorically rehearsing his regression, death, and rebirth. When his father finally succumbs to his long illness, Gerald feels himself writhing "on the edge of the chasm, suspended in chains of invisible physical life" and worries that he "could not fall into this infinite void, and rise again" (337). Nevertheless, this is exactly what he does. Two days after the funeral, he is seized by some mysterious force, stumbling and feeling his way through the woods "automatically" and "without thought or sensation" (338). This is not the automatism of the colliers, but the transcendent instinct of blood knowledge—*automatic* in the sense of "self-generated, spontaneous" and "without conscious thought" instead of the antonymic "works by itself under fixed conditions" (*OED*). When he emerges from the darkness and the woods, he passes through an "outlet," much like a newborn (338).[26] The destruction of the father has caused the rebirth of the man, who is now attuned in proper Lawrencian manner to sensation rather than intellect. He descends into the churchyard where his father is buried and, even in the darkness, sees "the heaped pallor of old white flowers at his feet"

[24] This reading is in conflict with Andrew Harrison's, which places a greater positive value on Lawrence's (admittedly ambiguous) relationship to Futurism, arguing that it "acted as a focus of ideas for Lawrence, satisfying a youthful desire for the sloughing off of pessimism and dead tradition whilst allowing him indirect access to the assimilated artistic energies" (xix). For Harrison, Lawrence "turned to Futurist vocabulary" in his articulation of the "destructive-consummating energies of war." Harrison, *D.H. Lawrence and Italian Futurism*, 111.

[25] Charles L. Ross, *Women in Love: A Novel of Mythic Realism* (Twayne Publishers, 1991), 136.

[26] The place-name raises a question that the place itself answers: what is more is this communion with the mystery, the mystery that suggests resurrection after death.

and smells "a raw scent of chrysanthemums and tube-roses, deadened" (338). Chrysanthemums and their scent had long symbolized death for Lawrence—most notably in "Odour of Chrysanthemums" (1911)—but in *Women in Love*, flowers and flowering take on a more complex meaning, symbolizing death as a precondition for life. At the beginning of the novel, for example, Gerald's sister arrives at her wedding in a carriage, emerging from "a shower of fine foliage and flowers" (18). Superficially, this appears to be a flurry of fertile imagery, but despite the restorative associations of *shower*, a flower that is *showering* or *falling* is a flower that is dying. Metaphors of life demand literal death. Meanwhile, her father stands nearby, "self-obliterated" (18). The rise of the new generation means the fall of the old—the argument of "Love and Death" itself—and for any parent the wound is self-directed. Likewise, at the graveyard, it is the smell of the chrysanthemums and tuberoses, killed for the purpose of commemoration, that stuns Gerald into action. Repulsed by their raw, deadened scent, he turns to Gudrun, the source of his rebirth.[27]

The journey to her home is one from darkness to light, a reflection of his own spiritual enlightenment: he walks past "dark shops" and ends in "a field of darkness," hesitating before approaching her house as it, too, may be "closed in darkness" (340). He has nothing to fear: he soon sees "a big lighted window" and the door "shedding a soft, coloured light from the hall lamp." Inside, in a suggestion that he is communing with blood knowledge, Gerald is described in mystical terms that favor touch over thought: "[He] stood a second suspended [...] His senses were so finely, almost supernaturally keen, that he seemed to cast his own will over the half-unconscious house" (341). While "half-unconscious" refers to the sleeping residents, it also applies to Gerald's semi-somnambulant state: "With an almost occult carefulness [...] he seemed to create a silence about himself, an obliviousness." He is still motivated by will, but a will that precedes *and* supersedes cognition, a will that directs him toward oblivion. This is what Birkin, above, calls the need to "lapse out before you can know what sensual reality is, lapse into unknowingness, and give up your volition." Gerald enters her brother's room by accident—a nod to his recent failure to undergo transformation through friendship with Birkin in "Gladiatorial"—and continues, once again, toward a "door afar" and its "faint light." Like a child

[27] Later, Hermione, no doubt parroting Birkin, uses the flower to demonstrate what is lost in the trade of innocence for enlightenment: "If I know about the flower, don't I lose the flower and have only the knowledge? Aren't we exchanging the substance for the shadow, aren't we forfeiting life for this dead quantity of knowledge?" (41).

being born, he is blind, deprived of all but his "tactile sense [… f]eeling his way forward with the tips of his fingers" and relying on his alert, "preternaturally fine senses" to find Gudrun's bedroom (342).

Upon reaching her, "his outstretched hand touched her warm breast." Sex heals him, and frequently the pair are figured as mother and child. The following passage abounds in allusions to the womb and amniotic fluid, to baptism and the creative fire of the phoenix:

> He was whole again […] he plunged deeper into her enveloping soft warmth, a wonderful creative heat that penetrated his veins and gave him life again. He felt himself sinking to rest in a bath of her living strength […] His blood, which seemed to have been drawn back into death, came ebbing on the return, surely, beautifully, powerfully […] He was a man again, strong and rounded. And he was a child, so soothed and restored and full of gratitude […] Mother and substance of all life she was [… T]he miraculous, soft effluence of her breast suffused over him […] like a soft, soothing flow of life itself, perfect as if he were bathed in the womb again.
>
> (344)

Once finished, "He buried his small, hard head between her breasts," a sly coupling of death (*buried*) and life (*breasts*) but also an indication that mental concerns, residing in the head, are being laid to rest (345). Drained of Thanatos, he sleeps "the sleep of complete exhaustion and restoration."

There is a cost to this restoration, a victim of his rebirth. While still beside the grave, a "dangerous resolve formed in his heart […] he could get at her—he *would* get at her […] if it cost him his life" (339; emphasis in original). Like the bride and bridegroom in "Eloi, Eloi," the roles of murderer and murdered are shared by both partners: Gerald is willing to risk his life, but the language more frequently suggests violence toward Gudrun. He drags the mud and clay from the churchyard into her room—she worries he may have left footprints—and in a reversal of the romantic cliché, "His heart did not beat" (342). His undressing sounds like "pistol-shots," the sex itself like a slow-motion bullet piercing her soul:

> Into her he poured all his pent-up darkness and corrosive death […] And she, subject, received him as a vessel filled with his bitter poison of death […] The terrible frictional violence of death filled her, and she received it in an ecstasy of subjection, in throes of acute, violent sensation.
>
> (344)

Gerald reaches blood knowledge at the price of condemning Gudrun to mental knowledge. He lies in "perfect sleep" while she remains awake, "destroyed into perfect consciousness [...] an exhausting super-consciousness" (345 and 346). Worst of all, she is damned to "automatic consciousness," or the obsessive fixation on mental concerns: "all the happenings she had not understood, pertaining to herself, to her family, to her friends, her lovers, her acquaintances, everybody." Her entire life. The man who once represented escape from the colliers' automatism has only achieved that freedom for himself. This is the creative destruction of "Eloi, Eloi," sublimated into a murderous impulse.

"Death and Love" is just a dress rehearsal. "Snowed Up" is a live performance. Lawrence begins the chapter with Gudrun and Loerke picnicking in the snow, sharing "some mocking dream of the destruction of the world by a ridiculous catastrophe of man's invention" (453). This is the same dream that was shared by Birkin and Ursula, but here it is warped into the replica Gudrun begins the novel condemning; it has become a fashionable bohemian provocation rather than a sincere expression of the death drive. Gerald appears as if from nowhere, at first seeming "a vague white figure," a description that circles back to his first appearance as "an arctic thing" (470). His voice sounds out "like a judgment in the whitish air of twilight," but when Loerke cries, "You come like a ghost!" he does not answer. Living in the liminal space between life and death, he is now a mixture of otherworldly apparition and otherworldly silence.

One last time, Gerald and Gudrun play murderer and murdered: after he tosses aside Loerke, she clenches her fist and brings it down on him. The violence stuns Gerald into recognition: "Wide, wide his soul opened, in wonder, feeling the pain [...] at last to take the apple of his desire" (471). The apple here evokes the fall of man. Scott Sanders has made the argument that *Lady Chatterley's Lover* (1928) reads as "an inverted form of the Eden myth," and much the same could be said of *Women in Love*.[28] The novel is a restoration myth, one that pairs sexuality and violence in a manner that demands death in return for spiritual resurrection. Rather than "Adam and Eve [...] cast back *into* the garden," it takes as its subject the force that casts them there (ibid.; emphasis in original). The cost of admission is blood, and Gerald's desire, for now, is to strangle Gudrun:

> He could feel the slippery chords of her life. And this he crushed, this he could crush. What bliss! Oh what bliss, at last, what satisfaction, at last! [...]

[28] Scott Sanders, *D.H. Lawrence: The World of the Five Major Novels* (Viking, 1973), 200. All subsequent references are noted parenthetically in the text.

> what a god-given gratification, at last! He was unconscious of her fighting and struggling. That struggling was her reciprocal lustful passion in this embrace, the more violent it became, the greater the frenzy of delight, till the zenith was reached, the crisis, the struggle was overborne, her movement became softer, appeased.
>
> (471–2)

The scene overflows with erotic language. Rhythmically it mimics the choreography of sex, beginning with longer sentences before turning to a series of staccato phrases culminating in a "zenith." In order to achieve the spiritual revelation sex offers, partners must first engage in a violent confrontation of opposing forces: the use of the word *crisis* as a euphemism for orgasm demonstrates how wrought with "struggle" Lawrence found the act. Consequently, orgasm and lifelessness are indistinguishable, Gudrun's "softer, appeased" movements ambiguous enough to indicate either the refractory period or unconsciousness. While sex is always deathly, so too is death always sexual, creative. At first glance, for example, the "slippery chords of her life" refer to Gudrun's vocal cords. The spelling suggests otherwise: Gerald's murderous impulse, and the instrumentality of her body, her vocal "chords," create a kind of music. Creation as the fruits of destruction.

Like the speaker in "Eloi, Eloi," Gerald turns his destructive instinct from the other to the self. After the body has been found, Birkin interprets his suicide as a creative violence. He is, admittedly, repulsed by Gerald's body, "the frozen carcase of a dead male," and his anatomical language mocks the paltry explanations of mental knowledge (477). Nevertheless, he is able to glimpse the outline of divine purpose: "Whatever the mystery which has brought forth man and the universe, it is a non-human mystery, it has its own great ends, man is not the criterion" (478). Birkin has heard the suicide's call. The death is like that of the mastodons: God is free to dispense with any species that has "failed to creatively develop," and why would this exclude humans? In their place will rise new generations, "new races and new species," perhaps even "new forms of consciousness" (479). While considering Lawrence's "utopian vision," Erwin Rosinberg writes that in "trying to access and represent worlds of experience beyond the confines of the world as it is, both Birkin and Lawrence must rely heavily on a language of negation."[29] I would suggest that Gerald's death is one such representation through negation, perhaps its quintessential expression.

[29] Erwin Rosinberg, "'After Us, Not Out of Us': Wrestling with the Future in D.H. Lawrence's *Women in Love*," *Modern Fiction Studies* 59, no. 1 (Spring 2013), 5.

Vibrating with such a consciousness, Gerald recreates his walk from the graveyard to Gudrun's bed in "Death and Love," though this time the suicide is literal and the rebirth unwritten. Again stumbling through the landscape, Gerald is driven to a single purpose: "He wanted to go on and on, to the end. Never again to stay, till he came to the end, that was all the desire that remained to him" (472). *Desire* recalls "the apple of his desire," reinforcing the sense that, like the apple in this inverted Eden, his desire for death will lead to the creation of a new world, ascended rather than fallen. Hence the mountain, which Gerald climbs spotting "the vague shadow of something higher" and thinking to himself, "Always higher, always higher" (473). The word *unconscious*, as in "unconsciously climbing" and even "he was not really conscious," peppers the final pages—just as he did in "Death and Love," Gerald is submitting to blood knowledge, and his body has entered a trance-like state that has no use for mental knowledge (472 and 473). Gerald simply wants to "keep going, until it was finished." His last words are, "I've had enough—I want to go to sleep. I've had enough" (472). Sleep, earlier associated with his restoration, has long been a seductive metaphor for death.

Gerald is motivated by outside forces as well. The mountain he climbs, with "*fallen* masses of rock and *veins* of snow *slashing* vaguely in and about," echoes two common means of suicide, a deep wrist injury and jumping from a dangerous location (emphasis added). Even the weather colludes with his underlying desire, and when he stands near a cliff, "very much afraid of falling, very much afraid of falling [… there] moved a wind that almost overpowered him with a sleep-heavy iciness" (473). Intuiting divine purpose, he knows he is supposed to fall elsewhere: "Only it was not here, the end, he must still go on." Like many a prophet, he resists the suicidal martyrdom he has been assigned. In addition to his fear of falling, Gerald dreads being murdered, and after strangling Gudrun, Lawrence's free indirect discourse asks, almost pleads, "Must he see, must he know?" (472). Ultimately, blood knowledge overpowers mental knowledge, and we read that his dread is a kind that "stood outside him, like his own ghost" (473). In fact, the chapter as a whole stands outside Gerald, too: his actions are described in detail, but there are few references to affective states, despite the impending suicide. In suspending his consciousness, Lawrence has also suspended his voice.

Regressing into animality, Gerald "slither[s] down a sheer snow-slope" and "sheer[s] away" from a crucifix half-buried in the snow, failing to reach the nearby Marienhütte, literally "Mary Hut." Still, the half-buried cross mirrors his own snowy martyrdom, which functions as a northern counterpart to Christ's crucifixion. Gerald asks, "Lord Jesus, was it then bound to be—Lord Jesus?" the phrasing of which allows for two possible readings: he is either asking Christ if he is "bound" to his death or asking an unnamed, apostrophic subject if *he* is "bound to be—Lord Jesus." In the theology of *Women in Love*, the latter interpretation is plausible, but as the word *slither* suggests, Lawrence was never himself bound to any single symbolic order, and the novel is also full of scientific metaphor: "Characters appear as solids, liquids and gases; they are likened to mud, clay, steel, radium and bronze," writes Sanders, and "under the stress of violent emotions, persons tend to dissolve into lumps of matter or lines of force, interacting by means of electricity, magnetism, friction, radio-activity or gravitation" (100).

Read in these terms, Gerald's suicide is not martyrdom but a transference of energy, which of course is another form of destructive creation. As Spielrein reminds her readers, "During reproduction, a union of female and male cells occur. The unity of each cell thus is destroyed and, from the product of this destruction, new life originates" (156). Earlier in the novel, Birkin uses an older, natural metaphor, claiming that "humanity never gets beyond the caterpillar stage—it rots in the chrysalis," paraphrasing Lawrence's argument in *Thomas Hardy* that we are "dying chrysalides," too afraid to leave our shells (128). Here, I would argue, Gerald has slithered and hardened into a healthy chrysalis, preparing for metamorphosis. For Lawrence, in this metaphor, the butterfly represents freedom through blood knowledge: the third panel of the triptych. In each iteration—as martyr, as energy, as larva—Gerald represents the self-destruction that causes creation.

Unfortunately for the reader, and for all who remain committed to mental knowledge as a central means of understanding the universe, the substance of this experience is untranslatable into language. Lawrence will never, indeed *can* never, write the butterfly. He can only gesture toward it. Sanders calls this the "paradox [that] lies at the heart of all Lawrence's work: he could only use verbal means to explore those dimensions of experience which, he maintained, were incompatible with language" (30). Once Gerald has frozen into the northern fetish statue, blood knowledge disappears with him. The description of his death is uncharacteristically succinct:

> He had come to the hollow basin of snow, surrounded by sheer slopes and precipices, out of which rose a track that brought one to the top of the mountain.

> But he wandered on unconsciously, till he slipped and fell down, and as he fell something broke in his soul, and immediately he went to sleep.
>
> (474)

There is a fairy-tale simplicity to the language here, and elsewhere Lawrence would have produced reams of words in place of "something broke in his soul." Through Gerald's death, sleep reconciles its restorative and suicidal connotations: in snow-abstract annihilation, he has gained the ultimate, final, and supreme blood knowledge. The reader can only peek over his shoulder.

Suicide discourse was dominated by two disciplines in the twentieth century: sociology and psychology. This was "the time of Freud and Durkheim."[30] Like the sociologists, Freud does not investigate the effects of suicide but its causes. For Freud, voluntary death is a question of etiology. In *Beyond the Pleasure Principle*, he argues that the cause of self-destruction is the death drive, "*an urge inherent in organic life to restore an earlier state of things*." Since nonexistence is the earliest state, "*the aim of all life is death*." In *Civilization and Its Discontents*, his remarks about happiness ("we should be much happier if we gave it up and returned to primitive conditions") seem to suggest, in their evocation of the death drive, that suicide might be a solution to the inevitable neuroses and misery of life among the civilized. Lawrence is more polemical, and in *Women in Love* he provides both the moral argument and the model. Unlike Freud, he does appear to be concerned with the effects of suicide, with the purposes it serves, and in this sense, he represents a return to the teleological explanations of the nineteenth century. The problem is that the twentieth-century Lawrence does not hold faith in their means of expression, and the limitations of language veil the answers to teleological questions in mysticism. Condemned to use the tools of his profession, he resigns himself to the causes of suicide. Ultimately, Lawrence remains on our side of the fence; he can only paint the first and second panels of his triptych.

[30] Margaret Pabst Battin, ed., *The Ethics of Suicide: Historical Sources* (Oxford University Press, 2015), 476.

Conclusion

When Queen Victoria inherited the throne in 1837, the English viewed suicide as a public event. A variety of discourses, most available to the amateur reader, shaped the debates on the subject. These debates often focused on its consequences: the burial outside the churchyard, the forfeiture of assets, perhaps even the final resting place of the soul. Juries were tasked with determining whether accidental deaths were cases of self-murder, and the press reported suicides and suicide notes alongside news of divorces and bankruptcies. In this context, Victorian fiction avoided what Andrew Bennett calls "the phenomenology, the lived experience [...] of suicide."[1] Instead, suicidal characters were often marginal, their deaths significant more for their effects than their causes. I call this phenomenon *the teleology of suicide*. Toward the end of the century, however, Marie Corelli and Robert Louis Stevenson used the "well established [...] literary subgenre" of the suicide note to explore the voices of suicidal characters up to the moment of self-destruction, offering readers an over-the-shoulder view of an action that, due to an ongoing cultural shift in meaning, was not quite villainous and not quite good.[2]

By the time Victoria died in 1901, teleological explanations were no longer tenable. The professionalization of death, the receding importance of juries, the abolition of laws and the relaxation of punishments, the decreased coverage in the press, all contributed to "a conspiracy of silence and willed ignorance" around voluntary death.[3] One major modernist response was to treat suicide

1 Andrew Bennett, *Suicide Century: Literature and Suicide from James Joyce to David Foster Wallace* (Cambridge University Press, 2017), 4.

2 Michael MacDonald and Terence R. Murphy, *Sleepless Souls: Suicide in Early Modern England* (Clarendon Press, 1990), 326.

3 Alan Warren Friedman, *Fictional Death and the Modernist Enterprise* (Cambridge University Press, 1995), 61.

as a problem of epistemology, a failure of knowing. Once causes, rather than effects, are contested, they become fertile narrative ground. Examples include John Galsworthy's *The Man of Property* (1906) and Ford Madox Ford's *The Good Soldier* (1915). Virginia Woolf, who observed the "conspiracy of silence" for most of her career, broke it once, in *Mrs. Dalloway* (1925), her first sustained experiment with stream-of-consciousness. By entering the mind of Septimus Warren Smith, a suicidal, shell-shocked war veteran, Woolf tested the limits of the formal tools of modernism and provided a counterpoint to the view of suicide as an epistemological failure.

In the twentieth century, suicide discourse was dominated by two disciplines: sociology and psychology. The "time of Freud and Durkheim" shifted the professional debates from the effects of suicide to its causes.[4] Durkheim asks what type of person kills themselves. Freud asks what motivates an individual to choose death. Writers of Golden Age detective fiction, a genre that relies on type, adopted the sociological model of voluntary death with greater readiness and fewer qualifications than its progenitors. D. H. Lawrence, on the other hand, wrestled with the suicidal implications of the death drive, a neurosis that could also be a cure. For Lawrence, suicide is once more a matter of teleology; the problem is that the teleological explanation cannot be articulated within the bounds of language. So he is left, like his contemporaries, to dissect the causes.

[4] Margaret Pabst Battin, ed., *The Ethics of Suicide: Historical Sources* (Oxford University Press, 2015), 476.

Bibliography

Abdalla, Venetia. "*The Good Soldier*: A Tale of Poison. Lethal Little Bottles in the Work of Ford Madox Ford and Violent Hunt." In *Ford Madox Ford's The Good Soldier: Centenary Essays*, edited by Max Saunders and Sara Haslam. Brill, 2015, 197–212.

Abel, Elizabeth. *Virginia Woolf and the Fictions of Psychoanalysis*. The University of Chicago Press, 1993.

"An Act to Alter and Amend the Law Relating to the Interment of the Remains of Any Person Found *Felo de se*." July 8, 1823.

Adams, John. "An Essay Concerning Self-Murther." In *The Ethics of Suicide*, edited by Margaret Pabst Battin. Oxford University Press, 2015, 384–6.

Allinghan, Margery. *The Fashion in Shrouds*. Manor Books, 1976.

Alvarez, A. *The Savage God: A Study of Suicide*. Penguin, 1974.

Améry, Jean. *On Suicide: A Discourse on Voluntary Death*. Translated by John D. Barlow. Indiana University Press, 1999.

Anderson, Olive. *Suicide in Victorian and Edwardian England*. Oxford University Press, 1987.

Aquinas, Thomas. "Summa Theologica." In *The Ethics of Suicide*, edited by Margaret Pabst Battin. Oxford University Press, 2015, 227–30.

Ariès, Philippe. *The Hour of Our Death*. Translated by Helen Weaver. Barnes & Noble Books, 2000.

Augustine. *City of God*. Translated by Henry Bettenson. Penguin, 2004.

Baechler, Jean. *Suicides*. Translated by Barry Cooper. Basil Blackwell, 1979.

Bailey, Victor. *"This Rash Act": Suicide Across the Life Cycle in the Victorian City*. Stanford University Press, 1998.

Battin, Margaret Pabst, editor. *The Ethics of Suicide: Historical Sources*. Oxford University Press, 2015.

Belsey, Catherine. "Re-reading the Great Tradition." In *Re-reading English*, edited by Peter Widdowson. Routledge, 2003, 121–35.

Bennett, Andrew. *Suicide Century: Literature and Suicide from James Joyce to David Foster Wallace*. Cambridge University Press, 2017.

Berman, Jeffrey. *Surviving Literary Suicide*. University of Massachusetts Press, 1999.

Bethea, Arthur F. "Septimus Smith, the War-Shattered Christ Substitute in *Mrs. Dalloway*." *The Explicator* 68, no. 4 (2010): 249–52.

The Bible: Authorized King James Version with Apocrypha. Edited by Robert Carroll and Stephen Prickett. Oxford University Press, 2008.

Blackstone, William. "Commentaries on the Laws of England." In *The Ethics of Suicide*, edited by Margaret Pabst Battin. Oxford University Press, 2015, 418–20.

Boccaccio, Giovanni. *The Decameron*. Edited and translated by G. H. McWilliam. Penguin, 1995.

de Bracton, Henry. "On the Laws and Customs of England." In *The Ethics of Suicide*, edited by Margaret Pabst Battin. Oxford University Press, 2015, 219–21.

Bronfen, Elisabeth. *Over Her Dead Body: Death, Femininity, and the Aesthetic*. University of Michigan Press, 1992.

Brontë, Charlotte. *Jane Eyre*. Edited by Sally Shuttleworth. Oxford University Press, 2008.

Brontë, Charlotte. *The Letters of Charlotte Brontë Volume Two: 1848–1851*. Edited by Margaret Smith. Oxford University Press, 2000.

Browne, Sir Thomas. *Religio Medici*. Andrew Crooke, 1642.

Browne, Sir Thomas. *Religio Medici*. Andrew Crooke, 1643.

Byron, Lord. *The Major Works*. Edited by Jerome J. McGann. Oxford University Press, 2008.

Cheng, Vincent J. "A Chronology of *The Good Soldier*." *English Language Notes* 24 (September 1986): 91–7.

Christie, Agatha. *And then There Were None*. Pocket Books, 1976.

Christie, Agatha. *Cards on the Table*. Dell, 1936.

Christie, Agatha. *Murder in the Mews and Three Other Poirot Cases*. Fontana, 1989.

Christie, Agatha. *Sparkling Cyanide*. HarperCollins, 1992.

Coleridge, Samuel Taylor. *The Complete Poems of Samuel Taylor Coleridge*. Edited by William Keach. Penguin, 1997.

Collins, Wilkie. *Armadale*. Edited by Catherine Peters. Oxford University Press, 2009.

Constantine, David. Introduction to *The Sorrows of Young Werther* by Johann Wolfgang von Goethe. Oxford University Press, 2012.

Corelli, Marie. *The Sorrows of Satan, or the Strange Experience of One Geoffrey Tempest, Millionaire: A Romance*. Oxford University Press, 1996.

Corngold, Stanley. Introduction to *The Sufferings of Young Werther* by Johann Wolfgang von Goethe. Norton, 2012.

Craps, Stef. "Virginia Woolf: 'Kew Gardens' and 'The Legacy.'" In *A Companion to the British and Irish Short Story*, edited by Cheryl Alexander Malcolm and David Malcolm. Wiley-Blackwell, 2008, 193–201.

Cuddy-Keane, Melba. *Virginia Woolf, the Intellectual, and the Public Sphere*. Cambridge University Press, 2003.

Dante. *The Divine Comedy Volume 1: Inferno*. Translated by Mark Musa. Penguin, 1984.

Davies, Christie and Mark Neal. "Durkheim's Altruistic and Fatalistic Suicide." In *Durkheim's Suicide: A Century of Research and Debate*, edited by W. S. F. Pickering and Geoffrey Walford. Routledge, 2000, 36–52.

DeMeester, Karen. "Trauma and Recovery in Virginia Woolf's *Mrs. Dalloway*." *Modern Fiction Studies* 44, no. 3 (Fall 1998): 649–68.

Dickens, Charles. *Bleak House*. Edited by Stephen Gill. Oxford University Press, 1998.

Dickens, Charles. *Nicholas Nickleby*. Edited by Paul Schlicke. Oxford University Press, 2009.

Durkheim, Émile. *Le Suicide*. Ancienne Librairie Germer Baillière, 1897.

Durkheim, Émile. *Les Règles de la Méthode Sociologique*. Librairie Félix Alcan, 1919.

Durkheim, Émile. *On Suicide*. Translated by Robin Buss. Penguin, 2006.

Durkheim, Émile. *The Rules of the Sociological Method and Selected Texts on Sociology and Its Method*. Translated by W. D. Halls. Free Press, 2013.

Eliot, George. *Daniel Deronda*. Edited by Graham Handley. Oxford University Press, 2014.

"EXTRAORDINARY SUICIDE," *The Morning Post*, August 11, 1893.

Felski, Rita. "Suspicious Minds." *Poetics Today* 32, no. 2 (Summer 2011): 215–34.

Fleming, Caleb. "A Dissertation upon the Unnatural Crime of Self-Murder." In *The Ethics of Suicide*, edited by Margaret Pabst Battin. Oxford University Press, 2015, 400–402.

Ford, Ford Madox. *The Good Soldier*. Edited by Martin Stannard. Norton, 2012.

Freud, Sigmund. *Beyond the Pleasure Principle*. Translated by James Strachey. Norton, 1989.

Freud, Sigmund. *Civilization and Its Discontents*. Translated by James Strachey. Norton, 1989.

Friedman, Alan Warren. *Fictional Death and the Modernist Enterprise*. Cambridge University Press, 1995.

Galsworthy, John. *The Forsyte Sage*. Edited by Geoffrey Harvey. Oxford University Press, 2008.

Galvan, Jill. "Corelli's Caliban in a Glass: Realism, Antirealism, and *The Sorrows of Satan*." *English Literature in Transition, 1880–1920* 57, no. 3 (2014): 335–60.

Gannon, Christiane. "Marie Corelli's *The Sorrows of Satan*: Literary Professionalism and the Female Author as Priest." *English Literature in Transition, 1880–1920* 56, no. 3 (2013): 374–95.

Garber, Marjorie. *Shakespeare After All*. Anchor Books, 2004.

Garrison, Elise P. *Groaning Tears: Ethical and Dramatic Aspects of Suicide in Greek Tragedy*. Brill, 1995.

Gates, Barbara T. *Victorian Suicide: Mad Crimes and Sad Histories*. Princeton University Press, 1988.

Gay, Peter. *Freud: A Life for Our Time*. Norton, 1998.

Gilbert, Sandra M. and Susan Gubar. *The Madwoman in the Attic: The Woman Writer and the Nineteenth-Century Imagination*. Yale University Press, 2000.

Gindin, James. *John Galsworthy's Life and Art: An Alien's Fortress*. Macmillan, 1987.

Giordano Jr., Frank. *"I'd Have My Life Unbe": Thomas Hardy's Self-destructive Characters*. University of Alabama Press, 1984.

Godwin, William. "Enquiry Concerning Political Justice." In *The Ethics of Suicide*, edited by Margaret Pabst Battin. Oxford University Press, 2015, 454–6.

Gordon, David J. "D.H. Lawrence's Dual Myth of Origin." *The Sewanee Review* 89, no. 1 (Winter 1981): 83–94.

Green, Paul D. "Doors to the House of Death: The Treatment of Suicide in Sidney's *Arcadia*." *The Sixteenth Century Journal* 10, no. 3 (Autumn 1979): 17–27.

Guth, Deborah. "Rituals of Self-Deception: Clarissa Dalloway's Final Moment of Vision." *Twentieth Century Literature* 36, no. 1 (Spring 1990): 35–42.

Halperin, John. *Trollope and Politics: A Study of the Pallisers and Others*. Macmillan, 1977.

Hardy, Thomas. *Jude the Obscure*. Edited by Patricia Ingham. Oxford University Press, 2002.

Hare, Cyril. *Suicide Excepted*. Perennial Library, 1983.

Harrison, Andrew. *D.H. Lawrence and Italian Futurism: A Study of Influence*. Rodopi, 2003.

Hey, Richard. "Dissertation on Suicide." In *The Ethics of Suicide*, edited by Margaret Pabst Battin. Oxford University Press, 2015, 441–3.

Hirsch, Gordon. "Frankenstein, Detective Fiction, and Jekyll and Hyde." In *Dr. Jekyll and Mr. Hyde After One Hundred Years*, edited by William Veeder and Gordon Hirsch. University of Chicago Press, 1988, 1–13.

Hite, Molly. *Woolf's Ambiguities: Tonal Modernism, Narrative Strategy, Feminist Precursors*. Cornell University Press, 2017.

Hollington, Michael. "Story, History, Allegory: Some Ironies of *Jude the Obscure* from a Benjamin Perspective." In *Thomas Hardy and Contemporary Literary Studies*, edited by Tim Dolin and Peter Widdowson. Palgrave Macmillan, 2004, 99–115.

The Holy Qur'an. Translated by Abdullah Yusuf Ali. Wordsworth, 2000.

Hood, Thomas. *Poems*. Henry Frowde, 1907.

Huxley, Aldous. *Brave New World*. Perennial Library, 1969.

Jacobus, Mary. "Sue the Obscure." *Essays in Criticism*, no. 25 (1975): 304–28.

James, Simon J. "Marie Corelli and the Value of Literary Self-Consciousness: *The Sorrows of Satan*, Popular Fiction, and *Fin-de-Siècle* Canon." *Journal of Victorian Culture* 18, no. 1 (2013): 134–51.

Jefferson, Thomas. *The Writings of Thomas Jefferson Volume XI*. Edited by Andrew A. Lipscomb. The Thomas Jefferson Memorial Association, 1904.

Johnson, Samuel. *A Dictionary of the English Language Volume II*. W. Strahan, 1855.

Joyce, James. *Ulysses*. Edited by Hans Walter Gabler, Wolfhard Steppe, and Claus Melchior. Vintage, 1986.

Jung, C. G. *Psychology of the Unconscious*. Translated by Beatrice M. Hinkle. Dover, 2002.

Keats, John. *The Major Works*. Edited by Elizabeth Cook. Oxford University Press, 2008.

Keene, Donald. "The Love Suicides at Sonezaki." In *Masterworks of Asian Literature in Comparative Perspective*, edited by Barbara Stoler. Routledge, 1994, 517–25.

Kershner, R. Brandon. "Corelli's Religious Trilogy: *Barabbas*, *The Sorrows of Satan*, and *The Master-Christian*." In *A Companion to Sensation Fiction*, edited by Pamela K. Gilbert. Wiley-Blackwell, 2011, 591–602.

Kinkead-Weekes, Mark. "Violence in *Women in Love*." In *D.H. Lawrence's Women in Love: A Casebook*, edited by David Ellis. Oxford University Press, 2006, 221–44.

Koretsky, Deanna P. *Death Rights: Romantic Suicide, Race, and the Bounds of Liberalism*. State University of New York Press, 2021.

Laird, Holly A. "Suicide in D.H. Lawrence's *Women in Love*: A Modernist Ethics." In *New D.H. Lawrence*, edited by Howard J. Booth. Manchester University Press, 2009, 59–79.

Lawrence, D. H. "The Future of the Novel." In *Study of Thomas Hardy and Other Essays*, edited by Bruce Steele. Cambridge University Press, 2002, 149–55.

Lawrence, D. H. *The Letters of D.H. Lawrence Volume II: June 1913–October 1916*. Edited by George J. Zytaruk and James T. Boulton. Cambridge University Press, 1981.

Lawrence, D. H. *The Letters of D.H. Lawrence Volume III: October 1916–June 1921*. Edited by James T. Boulton and Andrew Robertson. Cambridge University Press, 1984.

Lawrence, D. H. *The Letters of D.H. Lawrence Volume V: March 1924–March 1927*. Edited by James T. Boulton and Lindeth Vasey. Cambridge University Press, 1989.

Lawrence, D. H. *The Poems Volume III: Uncollected Poems and Early Versions*. Edited by Christopher Pollnitz. Cambridge University Press, 2018.

Lawrence, D. H. *Psychoanalysis and the Unconscious and Fantasia of the Unconscious*. Edited by Bruce Steele. Cambridge University Press, 2014.

Lawrence, D. H. *Study of Thomas Hardy and Other Essays*. Edited by Bruce Steele. Cambridge University Press, 2002.

Lawrence, D. H. *Women in Love*. Edited by David Farmer, Lindeth Vasey, and John Worthen. Cambridge University Press, 1987.

Lichtheim, Miriam, editor. *Ancient Egyptian Literature Volume I: The Old and Middle Kingdoms*. University of California Press, 1973.

Long, Orie W. "English Translations of Goethe's *Werther*." *The Journal of English and Germanic Philology* 14, no. 2 (April 1915): 169–203.

Lovesey, Oliver. "The Other Woman in *Daniel Deronda*." *Studies in the Novel* 30, no. 4 (Winter 1998): 505–20.

Lukes, Steven. Introduction to *The Rules of the Sociological Method and Selected Texts on Sociology and Its Method* by Émile Durkheim. Free Press, 2013.

Luther, Martin. "Table Talk." In *The Ethics of Suicide*, edited by Margaret Pabst Battin. Oxford University Press, 2015, 243–4.

MacDonald, Michael. "The Medicalization of Suicide in England: Laymen, Physicians, and Cultural Change, 1500–1870." *The Milbank Quarterly* 67 (1989): 69–91.

MacDonald, Michael and Terence R. Murphy. *Sleepless Souls: Suicide in Early Modern England*. Clarendon Press, 1990.

Malory, Sir Thomas. *Le Morte Darthur*. March 1469 to March 1470, MS 59678. The British Library, London.

Marcus, Laura. "The Short Fiction." In *A Companion to Virginia Woolf*, edited by Jessica Berman. Wiley Blackwell, 2016, 27–39.

Marinetti, F. T. "The Founding and Manifesto of Futurism." Translated by Lawrence Rainey. In *Futurism: An Anthology*, edited by Christine Poggi Rainey and Laura Wittman. Yale University Press, 2009, 49–53.

Martyr, Justin. "The Second Apology." In *The Ethics of Suicide*, edited by Margaret Pabst Battin. Oxford University Press, 2015, 150–1.

McGuire, Kelly. *Dying to Be English: Suicide Narratives and National Identity, 1721–1814*. Pickering & Chatto, 2012.

Meyer, Susan Lynn. *Imperialism at Home: Race and Victorian Women's Fiction*. University of Michigan Press, 1996.

Michalopoulos, Andreas N. "Lucius' Suicide Attempts in Apuleius' 'Metamorphoses.'" *The Classical Quarterly* 52, no. 2 (2002): 538–48.

Minois, Georges. *History of Suicide: Voluntary Death in Western Culture*. Translated by Lydia G. Cochrane. Johns Hopkins University Press, 1999.

Miyoshi, Masao. "Dr. Jekyll and the Emergence of Mr. Hyde." *College English* 27, no. 6 (March 1966): 470–4 and 479–80.

Montesquieu. "The Spirit of the Laws." In *The Ethics of Suicide*, edited by Margaret Pabst Battin. Oxford University Press, 2015, 392–6.

Murray, Alexander. *Suicide in the Middle Ages Volume II: The Curse on Self-Murder*. Oxford University Press, 2007.

Nicoletti, L. J. "Downward Mobility: Victorian Women, Suicide, and London's 'Bridge of Sighs.'" *Literary London: Interdisciplinary Studies in the Representation of London* 2, no. 1 (March 2004).

Nicoletti, L. J. "Morbid Topographies: Placing Suicide in Victorian London." In *A Mighty Mass of Brick and Smoke: Victorian and Edwardian Representations of London*, edited by Lawrence Phillips. Rodopi, 2007, 7–34.

Oliphant, Margaret. "The Anti-Marriage League." In *Thomas Hardy: The Critical Heritage*, edited by R. G. Cox. Routledge, 2005, 269–73.

Olk, Claudia. *Virginia Woolf and the Aesthetics of Vision*. De Gruyter, 2014.

Ovid. *Heroides*. Translated by Harold Isbell. Penguin, 1990.

Oxindine, Annette. "Rhoda Submerged: Lesbian Suicide in *The Waves*." In *Virginia Woolf: Lesbian Readings*, edited by Eileen Barrett and Patricia Cramer. New York University Press, 1997, 203–21.

Parisot, Eric. "Suicide Notes and Popular Sensibility in the Eighteenth-Century British Press." *Eighteenth-Century Studies* 47, no. 3 (Spring 2014): 277–91.

Pawlikowska, Kamila. *Anti-Portraits: Poetics of the Face in Modern English, Polish and Russian Literature (1835–1965)*. Brill, 2015.

Pepys, Samuel. "Diary." In *The Ethics of Suicide*, edited by Margaret Pabst Battin. Oxford University Press, 2015, 312–13.

Petrarch. *The Canzoniere or Rerum vulgarium framenta*. Translated by Mark Musa. Indiana University Press, 1999.

Phillips, Edward, editor. *The New World of English Words*. E. Tyler, 1658.

Plutarch. "Parallel Lives." In *The Ethics of Suicide*, edited by Margaret Pabst Battin. Oxford University Press, 2015, 127–8.

Pope, Alexander. *The Major Works*. Edited by Pat Rogers. Oxford University Press, 2006.

Pope, Whitney. *Durkheim's Suicide: A Classic Analyzed*. University of Chicago Press, 1976.

Pridmore, Saxby and Zainab Abd Majeed. "The Suicides of *The Metamorphoses*." *Australasian Psychiatry* 19, no. 1 (February 2011): 22–4.

Racine, Jean. *Britannicus; Phaedra; Athaliah*. Translated by C. H. Sisson. Oxford University Press, 2001.

Reynier, Christine. *Virginia Woolf's Ethics of the Short Story*. Palgrave Macmillan, 2009.

Rosenbaum, Ellen B. "Women's Speech and the Roles of the Sexes in *Daniel Deronda*." *Texas Studies in Literature and Language* 31, no. 2 (Summer 1989): 237–56.

Rosenthal, Lecia. *Mourning Modernism: Literature, Catastrophe, and the Politics of Consolation*. Fordham University Press, 2011.

Rosinberg, Erwin. "'After Us, Not Out of Us': Wrestling with the Future in D.H. Lawrence's *Women in Love*." *Modern Fiction Studies* 59, no. 1 (Spring 2013): 1–25.

Ross, Charles L. *Women in Love: A Novel of Mythic Realism*. Twayne Publishers, 1991.

Sager, Laura. "Septimus' Suicide." *Virginia Woolf Bulletin*, no. 3 (January 2000): 26–8.

"THE SAILOR SUICIDE AND SHAKESPEARE," *The Evening Telegraph*, February 3, 1898.

Sanders, Scott. *D.H. Lawrence: The World of the Five Major Novels*. Viking, 1973.

Sbaraini, Ella. "The Materiality of English Suicide Letters, c.1700–c.1850." *The Historical Journal* 65 (2022): 612–39.

Seneca. *Tragedies*. Translated by Frank Justus Miller. William Heinemann Ltd., 1938.

Sennett, Richard. Introduction to *On Suicide* by Émile Durkheim. Penguin, 2006.

Shakespeare, William. *The Norton Shakespeare*. Edited by Stephen Greenblatt, Walter Cohen, Suzanne Gossett, Jean E. Howard, Katharine Eisaman Maus, and Gordon McMullan. Norton, 2016.

Shikibu, Murasaki. *The Tale of Genji*. Translated by Dennis Washburn. Norton, 2016.

Showalter, Elaine. "Dr. Jekyll's Closet." In *The Haunted Mind: The Supernatural in Victorian Literature*, edited Elton E. Smith and Robert Haas. Lanham, 1999, 67–88.

Showalter, Elaine. "Syphilis, Sexuality, and the Fiction of the Fin de Siècle." In *Sex, Politics, and Science in the Nineteenth-Century Novel*, edited by Ruth Bernard Yeazell. Johns Hopkins University Press, 1986, 88–115.

Shuttleworth, Sally. *The Mind of the Child: Child Development in Literature, Science, and Medicine, 1830–1900*. Oxford University Press, 2010.

Smith, Andrew. "'The Body of a Self-Destroyer': Suicide and the Self in the *Fin-de-Siècle* Gothic." In *Suicide and the Gothic*, edited by William Hughes and Andrew Smith. Manchester University Press, 2019, 66–80.

Sophocles. *The Three Theban Plays*. Translated by Robert Fagles. Penguin, 1984.

Spielrein, Sabina. "Destruction as the Cause of Coming into Being." Translated by Kenneth McCormick. *Journal of Analytical Psychology* 39, no. 2 (1994): 155–86.

Spivak, Gayatri Chakravorty. "Three Women's Texts and a Critique of Imperialism." *Critical Inquiry* 12, no. 1 (1985): 243–61.

Steele, Bruce. Introduction to *Psychoanalysis and the Unconscious and Fantasia of the Unconscious* by D. H. Lawrence. Cambridge University Press, 2014.

Stevenson, Robert Louis. *Strange Case of Dr. Jekyll and Mr. Hyde*. Edited by Katherine Linehan. Norton, 2003.

Strahan, S. A. K. *Suicide and Insanity*. Swan Sonnenschein, and Co., 1893.

"SUICIDE," *The Jersey Weekly Press and Independent*, February 14, 1891.

"SUICIDE CATCHERS," *The Falkirk Herald and Midland Counties Journal*, November. 28, 1900.

"SUICIDE OF A CHILD: DOCTOR'S DAUGHTER ENDS HER LIFE," *The Evening Telegraph and Star*, August 7, 1897.

"A SUICIDE'S EXTRAORDINARY LETTER," *The Swindon Advertiser*, April 27, 1895.

"A SUICIDE'S LETTER," *Cardiff Times and South Wales Weekly News*, July 15, 1893.

"A SUICIDE'S LETTER TO THE CORONER: EXTRAORDINARY EPISTLE," *The Yorkshire Evening Post*, August 20, 1891.

Tanakh: The Holy Scriptures: New Translation According to the Traditional Hebrew Text. The Jewish Publication Society, 1988.

Tate, Trudi. "Mrs. Dalloway and the Armenian Question." *Textual Practice* 8, no. 3 (1994): 467–86.

Thackeray, William Makepeace. "Sorrows of Werther." In *The Humorous Poetry of the English Language, from Chaucer to Saxe*, edited by James Parton. Fields, Osgood & Company, 1870, 318–19.

Thomas, Ronald R. *Detective Fiction and the Rise of Forensic Science*. Cambridge University Press, 2003.

Todd, Janet. "Suicide and Biography." *Comparative Criticism* 25 (2004): 57–66.

Trollope, Anthony. *The Way We Live Now*. Edited by John Sutherland. Oxford University Press, 1999.

Vālmīki. *Rāmāyana*. Translated by Arshia Sattar. Rowman & Littlefield, 2018.

Varty, John. "Suicide, Statistics, and Sociology: Assessing Douglas' Critique of Durkheim." In *Durkheim's Suicide*, edited by W. S. F. Pickering and Geoffrey Walford. University of Chicago Press, 2006, 53–65.

Voltaire. *Candide*. Translated by Roger Pearson. Oxford University Press, 2006.

Voltaire. "Philosophical Dictionary." In *The Ethics of Suicide*, edited by Margaret Pabst Battin. Oxford University Press, 2015, 396–400.

Walker, Gordon K. "Father Time's Suicide Note in *Jude the Obscure*." *Nineteenth-Century Fiction* 22, no. 3 (1967): 298–300.

Wesley, John. "Thoughts on Suicide." In *The Ethics of Suicide*, edited by Margaret Pabst Battin. Oxford University Press, 2015, 403–4.

Westcott, Wynn. *Suicide: Its History, Literature, Jurisprudence, Causation, and Prevention*. H. K. Lewis, 1885.

Womack, Kenneth. "'It Is All a Darkness': Death, Narrative Therapy, and Ford Madox Ford's *The Good Soldier*." *Papers on Language & Literature* 38, no. 3 (Summer 2002): 316–33.

Woolf, Virginia. *Between the Acts*. Edited by Mark Hussey. Cambridge University Press, 2011.

Woolf, Virginia. *The Complete Shorter Fiction of Virginia Woolf*. Edited by Susan Dick. Harvest, 1989.

Woolf, Virginia. *The Diary of Virginia Woolf Volume One: 1915–1919*. Edited by Anne Olivier Bell. Harvest/HBJ, 1977.

Woolf, Virginia. *The Diary of Virginia Woolf Volume Two: 1920–1924*. Edited by Anne Olivier Bell. Harvest, 1978.

Woolf, Virginia. *The Essays of Virginia Woolf: Volume Three:1919–1924*. Edited by Andrew McNeillie. Harcourt, 1988.

Woolf, Virginia. *The Letters of Virginia Woolf Volume One: 1882–1912*. Edited by Nigel Nicolson and Joanne Trautmann. Harvest, 1975.

Woolf, Virginia. *The Letters of Virginia Woolf Volume Three: 1923–1928*. Edited by Nigel Nicolson and Joanne Trautmann. Harcourt Brace Jovanovich, 1978.

Woolf, Virginia. *The Letters of Virginia Woolf Volume Six: 1936–1941*. Edited by Nigel Nicolson and Joanne Trautmann. Harcourt Brace Jovanovich, 1980.

Woolf, Virginia. *Mrs. Dalloway*. Edited by Anne E. Fernald. Cambridge University Press, 2014.

Woolf, Virginia. *Orlando*. Edited by Suzanne Raitt and Ian Blyth. Cambridge University Press, 2018.

Woolf, Virginia. *A Passionate Apprentice: The Early Journals 1897–1909*. Edited by Mitchell A. Leaska. Harcourt Brace Jovanovich, 1990.

Woolf, Virginia. *A Room of One's Own*. Harvest, 2005.

Woolf, Virginia. *The Waves*. Edited by Michael Herbert and Susan Sellers. Cambridge University Press, 2011.

Wordsworth, William. *The Major Works*. Edited by Stephen Gill. Oxford University Press, 2008.

Index

Note: Page numbers followed by "n" refer to foot notes.

www.ingramcontent.com/pod-product-compliance
Ingram Content Group UK Ltd.
Pitfield, Milton Keynes, MK11 3LW, UK
UKHW021027041026
15470UKWH00013B/70

9 798765 128817